MARCO

TENERIFE

GOMERA AND HIERRO

with Local Tips
The author's special recommendations are highlighted in yellow throughout this guide

There are five symbols to help you find your way around this guide:

★

Marco Polo's top recommendations – the best in each category

☀

sites with a scenic view

◉

places where the local people meet

🧍

places where young people get together

(100/A1)
pages and coordinates for the Road Atlas

MARCO 🌐 POLO

Travel guides and language guides in this series:

Algarve • Amsterdam • Australia • Berlin • Brittany • California
Channel Islands • Costa Brava/Barcelona • Costa del Sol/Granada
Côte d'Azur • Crete • Cuba • Cyprus • Eastern USA • Florence • Florida
Gran Canaria • Greek Islands/Aegean • Ibiza • Ireland • Istanbul • Lanzarote
London • Mallorca • Malta • New York • New Zealand • Normandy • Paris
Prague • Rhodes • Rome • Scotland • South Africa • Southwestern USA
Tenerife • Turkish Coast • Tuscany • Venice • Western Canada

French • German • Italian • Spanish

Marco Polo would be very interested to hear your comments and suggestions. Please write to:

North America:
Marco Polo North America
70 Bloor Street East
Oshawa, Ontario, Canada
(B) 905-436-2525

United Kingdom:
GeoCenter International Ltd
The Viables Centre
Harrow Way
Basingstoke, Hants RG22 4BJ

Our authors have done their research very carefully, but should any errors or omissions have occurred, the publisher cannot be held responsible for any injury, damage or inconvenience suffered due to incorrect information in this guide

Cover photograph: Mauritius: Kahlbrandt + Kahlbrandt
Photos: Baumli (12, 22, 28, 32, 50, 66, 72); Kallabis (62); Lade: BAV (41); Lindner (16);
Mauritius: Beck (48), Hubatka (99), Leblond (7, 77), Mehlig (8), Murillo (83), Nägele (55),
Pigneter (4), Schwanke (30); Nowaczyk (14); Schapowalow: Huber (85); Transglobe: Merten (69, 71), Mollenhauer (90), Svensson (27); Touristik-Marketing GmbH (34)

2nd revised edition 2000
© Mairs Geographischer Verlag, Ostfildern, Germany
Authors: Dieter Nowaczyk and Hannelore Lindner
Translator: Dennis Brehme
English edition 2000: Gaia Text
Editorial director: Ferdinand Ranft
Chief editor: Marion Zorn
Cartography for the Road Atlas: © Mairs Geographischer Verlag
Design and layout: Thienhaus/Wippermann
Printed in Germany

All rights reserved. No part of this publication may be reproduced or transmitted in any form or by any means, electronic or mechanical including photocopying, recording or by any information storage and retrieval systems without prior permission from the publisher

CONTENTS

Introduction: Discover Tenerife! **5**
Where the sea and the mountains, the lush tropical vegetation and the desert combine to create an island full of charm and contrasts

History at a glance **6**

Tenerife in context: Guanches and dragon trees **13**
The largest of the Canary Islands boasts a wealth of natural beauty, including Spain's highest mountain

Food & drink: Canarian cuisine **23**
Hearty stews, home-grown vegetables and plenty of delicious fresh fish make for simple, yet very tasty local fare

Shopping & souvenirs: Woodcarvers and lacemakers **29**
Markets in the towns and villages regale the senses with colourful sights and mouth-watering smells

Events: Carpets of flowers **31**
With festivals and carnivals all year round, the inhabitants of Tenerife certainly know how to celebrate

The north-west coast: Paradise on earth **35**
Historic towns and charming fishing villages nestle amongst banana plantations and vineyards

The north-east coast: Cliffs and chasms **51**
Hikers will be rewarded with some stunning views in this rugged part of the island

National park: A lunar landscape **63**
This spectacular volcanic backdrop took shape more than a quarter of a million years ago

The south-east coast: Rugged beauty **67**
The rural, unspoilt side of Tenerife lies to the east of the Teide

The south-west coast • Gomera • Hierro: A holiday haven **73**
A haven for beach-lovers and water-sports enthusiasts

Routes on Tenerife **86**

Essentials: Practical information **91**
Important addresses and useful information for your visit to Tenerife

Do's and don'ts **98**

Road Atlas of Tenerife **99**

Index **119**

What do you get for your money? **120**

INTRODUCTION

Discover Tenerife!

*Where the sea and the mountains,
the lush tropical vegetation and the desert combine to create an
island full of charm and contrasts*

The largest and perhaps the most beautiful of the Canary Islands, Tenerife has everything the traveller needs to fulfil holiday dreams. It is an island of spectacular contrasts, with majestic volcanoes, vast banana plantations, stretches of desert, pine forests and fertile valleys interspersed with traditional villages, bustling towns and tourist resorts. The flat coastal plains, light sandy beaches, the blue Atlantic and the almost perpetual sun offer an irresistible year-round invitation. Whatever you're looking for in a holiday destination, you will find it here. The miles of coastline, plus some magnificent waves, make this spot ideal for watersports enthusiasts, while windsurfers and sailors head for the south of the island, where the wind is strong and steady. Sunworshippers and beach-lovers won't be disappointed either. There is rarely a cloud in the sky and the island is scattered with sandy beaches and isolated coves. For outdoor adventurers, there is a whole network of country paths and large areas of magnificent woodland to explore. The majestic mountains, cut through with wild and romantic gorges, are perfect for climbing. In the winter months, there's even snow at altitudes above 2,000 m (6,500 feet). And if this abundance of natural beauty isn't enough, Tenerife has an active nightlife, with plenty of opportunities to wind down after a hard day's worth of exploring or sunbathing. For night-owls, there's no shortage of clubs that stay open until the late hours.

Travellers flying into Tenerife for the first time will peer down from the tiny cabin window to catch a first glimpse of this volcanic island in the Atlantic – and may well be disappointed by what they see, or rather, don't see. Apart from a band of clouds hovering above the island, hardly any of its famous attractions are visible. Even after landing, you may look around and wonder whether you have accidentally arrived at the wrong place. After

*Tenerife's natural kaleidoscope
of colours, the unforgettable
'Island of Eternal Spring'*

History at a glance

1100–800 BC
The Phoenicians are probably the first people to set foot on the Canary Islands

1341
The islands are rediscovered by Portuguese seafarers

1402
Jean de Béthencourt sets out to conquer the archipelago for the Castilian crown

1477
The Catholic Kings charge Alonso Fernández de Lugo with the task of conquering the independent islands of Gran Canaria, Tenerife and La Palma

9 August 1492
Christopher Columbus, on his way to the New World, sails past the island and records the eruption of the Teide volcano

1494
Spaniards land on the beach of Azaña, now Santa Cruz. Peace negotiations with the Guanches fail

1495
The Spaniards defeat the Guanches at La Victoria. Tenerife is the last island to fall into Spanish hands

16th century
Tenerife is colonized and the Guanches are converted to Christianity. Sugar cane is cultivated and processed

17th century
Vineyards are planted after sugar cane turns out to be unprofitable

1704–06
Serious volcanic eruptions

1715
A crisis in the wine production forces many islanders to emigrate to Latin America

1744
La Laguna becomes the island's first college town

1797
Admiral Nelson loses his right arm during an attack on Santa Cruz

1852
The Canary Islands are divided into two provinces: Santa Cruz de Tenerife and Las Palmas de Gran Canaria

Since 1870
The success of aniline dyes causes the collapse of the local cochineal industry and forces thousands to emigrate once again

1888
First banana plantations

18 July 1936
Gen. Francisco Franco, the military commander of the Canary Islands, flees Santa Cruz to Spanish Morocco and starts the Spanish Civil War

Since 1960
Tourism becomes the leading sector of the Canarian economy

1982
The two Canary Island provinces become autonomous regions

INTRODUCTION

the four-hour flight from northern Europe's chilly climes, you emerge from the Reina Sofía airport looking at an arid landscape fringed by bare, volcanic peaks, where dusty cacti and parched shrubs bake under the hot sun. The vegetation has all the hallmarks of the Sahara Desert, which is only 300 km (186 miles) away. But don't feel dismayed – the golden beaches and crystal-clear waters are closer than they seem. The island's two main holiday centres, Playa de las Américas and Los Cristianos, the ultimate destinations for the majority of visitors, are only a few kilometres away from the airport, on the eastern side of the island's southern tip. Although not renowned for its scenery, the region does have its own appeal, though this has more to do with the superb water-sports facilities and the nightlife.

The road that heads due north from the airport hugs the coastline as it winds its way through a sandy, stony landscape, then veers westwards and suddenly, after just an hour's drive, the surroundings are miraculously transformed and you find yourself entering a wholly different natural environment. This side of the island is a kaleidoscope of colour, and one of outstanding natural beauty. Now you know why the island is referred to as the 'Island of Eternal Spring'. The lush green of of the banana plantations, the verdant woodland and an ever-changing variety of

Prickly pear cacti have flourished on Tenerife for centuries

multicoloured vegetation extend for miles across the northern half of Tenerife.

The central massif, called Cumbre Dorsal, is clearly visible as it emerges from the clouds. It divides the island into two distinct zones: the dry, barren south and the rich, fertile north. In the north, the sunny climate and mineral-rich soil, plus the gently north-easterly trade winds provide ideal conditions for an ever-abundant and diverse flora. The moist air blowing in from the ocean collides with the mountain tops, cooling as it rises. Consequently, along the northern slopes at altitudes lying between 700 and 1,700 m (2,300 and 5,600 feet), clouds form during the morning, usually dispersing by afternoon. However, these clouds rarely burst, and the vegetation receives its life-giving moisture in the form of mist and condensation. On the lee side of the mountains, the trade winds turn into dry, downhill drafts. These help to lower temperatures in the south, which would otherwise be two to four degrees Celsius higher. Nowhere else in the world do these unique climatic conditions exist. They bestow on the island well-balanced temperatures, which even in the summer range from 18 to 24°C (65 to 75°F), and in the winter average between 16 and 20°C (61 and 68°F), thus making Tenerife a perfect holiday destination at any time of the year. Even when the mercury rises, the heat is never very oppressive, as the constant trade winds help to reduce its intensity. In the evening, the air remains mild and pleasantly cool. Winter temperatures rarely drop below 14°C (57°F). It is no wonder that the explorer Anderson, a member of Captain Cook's third

Tall poinsettias line the island's paths and roads

INTRODUCTION

> **Time for a siesta**
>
> The Canary Islanders are not slaves to the clock — they are masters of it. Rushing around non-stop is not the Canarian way. Long queues at the post office or bank are a part of everyday life and holidaymakers are advised to exercise the same degree of patience as the islanders. In the more rural parts of the island, an afternoon siesta is still very much a part of the daily routine and this is the time when you will have to contend with the locals' relaxed attitude to life. Buses run late, churches and small museums close and bar-owners doze in front of their television screens. If you can adapt to this way of life, you will enjoy a more relaxing holiday than someone who insists on living the more stressful life of home.

expedition party, advised doctors to send their ailing patients to Tenerife to recuperate.

For many holidaymakers, the diversity of the landscape is one of Tenerife's main attractions. The bizarre lunar landscape above 2,000 m (6,500 feet) is captivating: congealed trails, blocks of lava in weird shapes and shimmering colours dominate the scenery, serving as an introduction to volcanology. Out of this strange and atmospheric setting rises Tenerife's highest mountain, the Pico del Teide (3,718 m / 12,200 feet), the highest peak on Spanish soil.

In north-eastern Tenerife the landscape suddenly changes and the unexpected contrast is quite breathtaking. This is where you find the fissured rocks of the Anaga mountain range, which forms a steep peninsula that rises up dramatically from the Atlantic. The Teno hills in the north-west are no less impressive. This tough, inaccessible world is blanketed with colourful plant life. Down in the valleys lie sleepy villages that reward the tourist who doesn't stick to the beaten track. For those looking for authentic Tenerife and who are willing to walk to find it, these areas represent the closest thing to paradise and are a good starting point for exploring the varied countryside. Along the island's north, the scenery unfolds and changes as if in a film: the stunning wilderness of the mountain region suddenly cuts to the bright green of a seemingly impenetrable woodland of laurel, eucalyptus, pines and firs. The fertile soil in the northern half of the island yields a rich harvest in the summer as well as in the winter. Cereals, tomatoes, potatoes, maize, grapes and many other kinds of fruit grow on the hillsides. Many fruits grow to a size that would make a self-respecting market gardener turn green with envy.

What is so fascinating about Tenerife is that, on a surface area of only 2,057 sq km (794 sq miles), as many different types of landscape occur as would normally be found on a continental land mass. Tenerife also boasts a number of indigenous plants and animals that don't grow anywhere else in the world. Red and violet bougainvillaea grow like weeds, brightening up house walls and street scenes, while the poinsettia, known to many Europeans as a Christmas pot plant, grows to a 4-m (13-foot)-high bush. Tourists impressed by the beauty of the strelitzia (the bird-of-paradise flower) can buy it as a present, ready-packed for the flight home. These floral marvels aren't just confined to the rural areas. They thrive everywhere and relieve the monotony of the concrete landscapes that prevail in many holiday resorts.

Observant travellers will enjoy exploring the artistic and architectural delights of the island's towns and villages. Traditional Canarian wooden balconies adorn many of Tenerife's original buildings. Other items of historic interest include art works and excavated artefacts that shed light on the island's history and its first inhabitants, the mysterious Guanches. What we do know is that these people were proud and peace-loving, characteristics that are still evident in today's *Canarios*, despite centuries of inbreeding since the arrival of the Spanish conquistadors. The *Canarios* are helpful and friendly; they are open and extremely hospitable. On this island, very few people regard punctuality as a virtue, and you should not let yourself become exasperated by what seems to be a stubborn indifference to time. The *Canarios* will treat foreigners differently depending on their social class, or whether they live in the towns or in the country. The more rural the setting, the more straightforward the islanders seem to be, particularly the older inhabitants who live their life at a different pace as they sit outside their front doors, impassive but satisfied with their lot and seemingly unaware of the rapid changes that have taken place in their world. It is no longer possible to ignore the lines of hotels in the south or in Puerto de la Cruz, the north's main resort. The relentless construction that mushroomed in the early 1960s drew increasing numbers of tourists with pockets full of hard currency to Puerto, and in just three decades its population has increased to about 27,000. The town has a cosmopolitan feel, characterized by a colourful blend of tourists and inhabitants from many different cultures, including *Canarios*, mainland Spaniards, Indian and Arab traders. Despite such radical changes, the old town retains some of its original charm in a maze of narrow streets and alleys and in its squares, where the locals enjoy siestas under the shade of the tall laurel trees and palms. The contrast is stark between the old and the new. Traditional Canarian houses with ornate wooden balconies and the old tranquil old fishing port, where anglers peacefully while away the hours, stand out against the brash hotels, throngs of tourists and traffic-jammed streets. But anyone who wishes to escape briefly from the hustle and bustle of thriving international tourism can easily find refuge in the nearby parks, flower gardens and other sanctuaries.

Tenerife also offers a wealth of entertainment and leisure activities for visitors in search of a

INTRODUCTION

break from the everyday work routine. And why on earth do three million foreigners, mainly northern Europeans, descend on this island each year? The enticing climate is certainly one reason, but there is more to Tenerife than the travel brochures can describe, more than the tour operators and travel agencies can provide. For many, this island has become something of a winter residence, which doesn't mean that Tenerife is suited only for senior citizens — quite the opposite. Young people find the island an ideal place for countless activities: every imaginable water sport, such as sailing, diving, windsurfing and waterskiing. Activities such as horseback riding, golf and tennis are as popular as walking or fishing. Those in search of a lively nightlife will certainly get their money's worth. In some resorts you'll even find English-language theatre productions; many hotels also put on cabarets for English-speaking guests. Throughout the year, locals from the neighbouring towns and villages stage a variety of festivals. Tenerife's original inhabitants revelled in song and dance and the descendants of the Guanches have added games and wrestling to these traditions. Characterized by lively rhythms and energetic dancing, the *Canarios'* festivals provide excellent opportunities for discovering the traditions and convivial nature of the islanders. The biggest and most colourful and extravagant of all the annual events is the Shrovetide Carnival, Mardi Gras, an occasion of such festivity that it could certainly rival the exuberance of its more famous counterpart in Rio.

Eventually, it becomes apparent that Tenerife's north has a drawback: it has no beaches. When the island was formed as a result of volcanic activity, the north coast was left with a steep, rocky shoreline that is, in most places, quite difficult to reach. In Puerto de la Cruz, however, two large beach areas have recently been made accessible — Playa Jardín and Playa Martiánez; near the latter there's an artificial seawater swimming pool. Other features along this stretch of coastline are the *barrancos*, gorges that cleave the hillsides as they come down to the sea. In the winter months, when the weather can turn very stormy, waves as high as houses thunder in, creating an impressive natural spectacle. Equally amazing (although in a completely different way) are the island's romantic sunsets, when the rocks are briefly bathed in glowing colour as the sun rapidly disappears beneath the Atlantic horizon.

Many visitors, especially the younger ones, find that Tenerife is an ideal base for island-hopping. You can catch a plane from the northern airport that will take you to the neighbouring islands of La Palma and Hierro in the west, or else take a ferry across to Gomera, the nearest island. If you have some spare time, try exploring the more barren, eastern islands of Gran Canaria, Lanzarote and Fuerteventura. By doing so, you will get a vivid impression of the astounding contrasts between each of the seven islands.

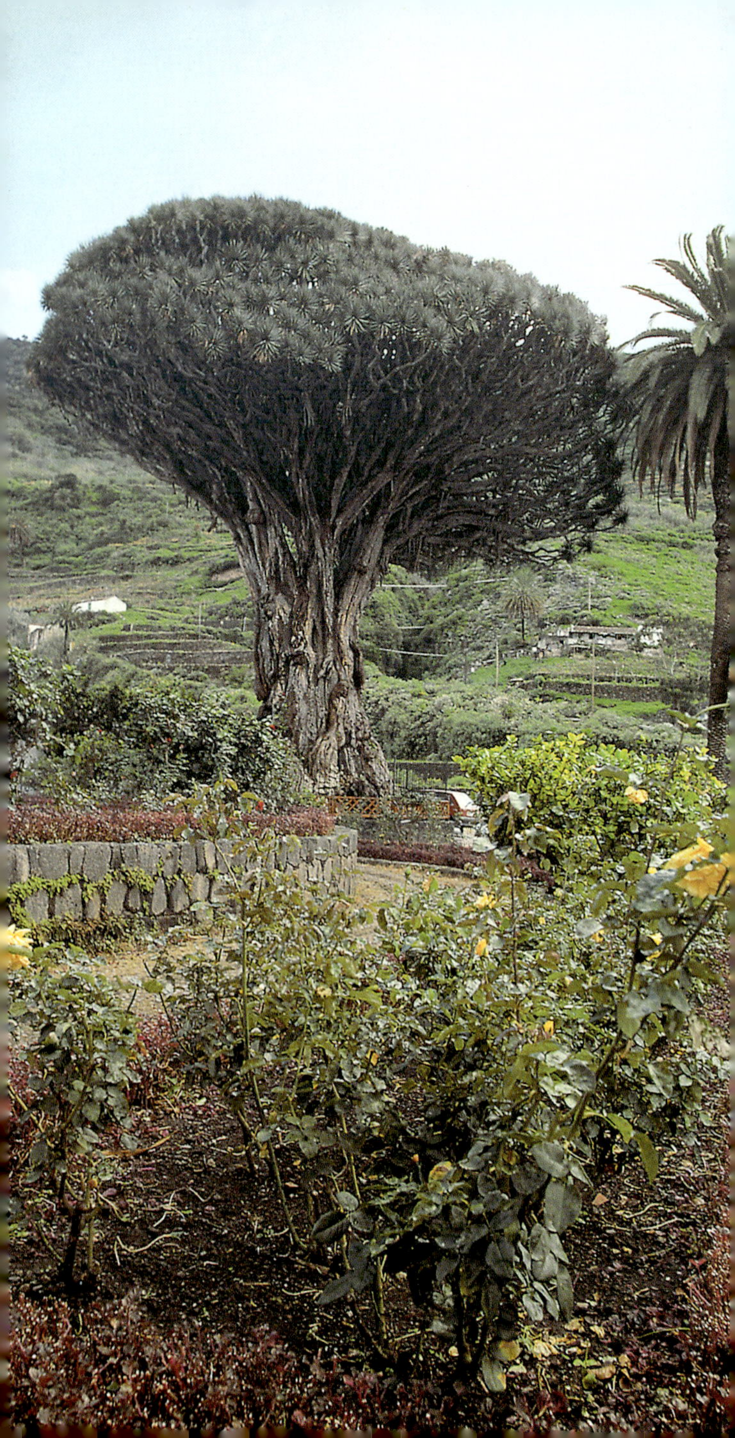

Guanches and dragon trees

The largest of the Canary Islands boasts a wealth of natural beauty, including Spain's highest mountain

Architecture

No destructive wars have taken place on Tenerife since the Spanish conquest, and owing to the mild climate, weather-related deterioration of buildings is minimal. As a result, many fine landowners' residences, churches, monasteries and houses from the 17th and 18th centuries have retained their original splendour. Soon after the island's conquest, the first churches appeared in Gothic style, but in the early 1600s immigrants from Andalusia and Portugal started building churches in the Mudéjar style. Visitors who explore the island thoroughly will discover that many churches were built during that period and the woodworkers' skills developed in parallel: ornately carved balconies, often from precious teak, which contrasts with the whitewashed walls, became a typical feature of house façades. The locals adopted the Spanish preference for building their houses around courtyards. Pretty gardens were laid out in these *patios*, which often included a fountain in the centre. The urban and rural poor built single-storey, white washed cottages, roofed with round red tiles, on a rectangular or L-shaped ground plan, sometimes, if they could afford it, with decorative carvings on doors and window frames. An irregular window arrangement usually indicates that the house was built in the 16th century; by the 17th century, a pattern of equal-sized windows with a door in the middle was becoming popular. In the early 19th century, Portuguese colonial-style Baroque with its elaborate cast-iron balconies appeared, mainly in the towns. Town halls and municipal buildings were erected in the Neoclassical style during this period. The mid-20th century saw the arrival of tourism and, unfortu-

Now cordoned-off for protection: the venerable dragon tree in Icod de los Vinos

nately, that also meant the hurried construstion of multi-storeyed concrete blocks. The 'Lago de Martiánez' sea-water swimming pools of Puerto de la Cruz, with islands and waterways, were designed by the Lanzarote artist and architect César Manrique in a style that blends with the contours of the natural surroundings. Nowadays, buildings in neo-Canarian style exhibit the traditional wooden balconies and decorative stonework.

Carpets of flowers
When in the mid-19th century interest in the Corpus Christi procession held in the Orotava valley waned, the aristocratic Señora del Castillo de Monteverde decided to revive the event by having a carpet of flowers laid in front of her house. Before long, a floral design with two doves suspended in the middle of an oval became the symbol of the procession. This colourful new art form quickly won many converts, and the tradition of lining the whole processional route with a carpet of blossoms was soon established. Some 150 carts were required to bring in the bales of heather used in the creation of those intricate floral patterns. By singeing the heather to varying degrees, it is possible to achieve various shades of colour, ranging from green to black. In this way, the backdrop to the picture is created, followed by the picture itself, consisting of various floral arrangements on top. When King Alfonso XIII visited La Orotava in March 1906, the town hall square was decorated with a carpet of blossoms for the first time ever. Felipe Machado y Benítez de Lugo soon became famous for his designs. He would start designing a month before Corpus Christi by integrating colourful pieces of lava soil into the picture. Dates, eucalyptus fruit, pieces of straw and vegetables were also included in the finished piece. His grandson Tomás conceived the idea of making a huge carpet measuring 870 square metres (9,365 square feet). Only one colour was used, but this colour changed in hue according to the direction of the light. Today, the municipal academy of art still lays out the three-part carpet in front of La Orotava's town hall, and every year thousands of visitors flock here to admire the biblical scenes that have been so painstakingly and skilfully created. A similar display can be seen at La Laguna,

An old, typical Tenerife house with carved wooden balconies

TENERIFE IN CONTEXT

where students lay out a floral carpet along the roads leading from La Concepción to the cathedral.

Geological origins

According to geological research carried out on the bedrock, the Anaga mountains in the north-east, the area around Adeje in the south-west and the Teno hills in the north-west are made up of basalt that is older than the rest of the island. Scientists have therefore concluded that these three regions were originally three separate islands, which gradually fused into one larger volcanic island some 6,000 m (19,700 feet) high. Further volcanic activity levelled off the summit at 2,000 m (6,500 feet), as seen in the present crater of Cañadas with a circumference of 45 km (28 miles). Further volcanic eruptions in the island's north-western edge created the Teide's volcanic cone by partially covering the even older volcanic deposits of the Pico Viejo. The last volcanic eruption took place in 1909, when Chinyero, north-west of Teide, spewed lava for ten consecutive days.

Folklore

On Tenerife, the veneration of a patron saint or the observation of a religious holiday is cause for celebration and that means, first and foremost, a solemn procession or a colourful parade. In the evening, jubilant music accompanied by dancing makes for a convivial gathering. Preparations start days in advance. The towns are decorated with brightly coloured garlands and a stage is erected on the plazas. *Tinerfeños*, as the islanders call themselves, don their colourful costumes when they set off on a *romería*, a pilgrimage – most of these take place between May and August – or when they are participating in an event organized for tourists. Every region has its own type of costume. In the Orotava valley, for example, the women wear a brightly coloured, striped dress gathered at the sides, with a richly embroidered bodice and a headscarf topped by a small straw hat. The music betrays clear South American influences and is played on large castanets *(chácaras)*, guitars, a type of mandolin *(banduria)* and the *timple*, a small guitar with four strings that produces evocative samba-like rhythms. In between, resonant songs showing Arabic influences and other lively ballads complete the repertoire. Rounds and other amusing dances are performed in groups, and some of the traditional sports are played out, much to the delight of the crowds. Activities include *lucha canaria*, a type of wrestling in which the object is to seize the turn-ups of the opponent's trousers and then floor him; *lucha de garrote*, a duel fought with sticks; *pulseo de piedra*, weight-lifting with lumps of rock and *salto del pastor*, in which shepherds jump across the *barrancos*.

Guanches

Virtually no traces survived of the Guanches, the first inhabitants of the Canary Islands and Tenerife, in particular; a few everyday objects and mummies are displayed in the museums and these artefacts constitute their only tangible remains. Many of the native islanders are proud of their Guanche roots, as this inheritance allows them to distance themselves from their Spanish conquerors. It is believed that there were two Guanche tribes: the Cro-Magnons and the Mediterraneans. The former was characterized by a wide face with coarse features, while the latter had a longer face with more delicate features. At that time, no links existed between the various islands, as there were no sailors. The peace-loving Guanches had many positive traits. Their king in Tenerife was referred to as the *mencey.* The death penalty was nonexistent but thieves were severely punished and a beating was meted out to anyone who behaved disrespectfully towards women. Murderers were deprived of their possessions, which were given to the relatives of the victims as compensation. The local economy was based on breeding cattle and cultivating crops, and local artisans used clay to make pottery and handsome, hand-painted utensils. Dwellings were either caves or stone huts roofed with straw. Clothes were made from tanned goat or sheepskin, while cheese and meat from goats or sheep, and *gofio*, roasted barley or wheat flour, were the staple foods, though they also ate fruit and fish, the latter caught with nets woven from rushes or palm leaves. The Guanches were monogamous; marriage required the agreement of both partners, but could be dissolved

Bronze statue of a Guanche king in Candelaria

at the request of either party. They believed in the existence of a higher being known as Aborac or Acoran. The dead were embalmed. Close examination of their language, customs, food and facial features points to a link with the Berbers of North Africa. Anthropologists strongly believe that the Guanches came from Barbery, in present-day Libya. How they made the journey remains a mystery.

African heat

Two to three times a year, nearly always in autumn and spring, a hot wind blows across to the Canary Islands from the Sahara, bringing rust-red sand and dust with it. The locals call this sirocco-like wind *el tiempo de África*. The heat reduces humidity on the island to almost zero and the temperature can rise to 40°C (104°F). The first

TENERIFE IN CONTEXT

signs of an approaching storm are wisps of reddish dust passing over the island's peaks. These particles get everywhere, into the tiniest cracks and crevices, but the wind gusts are the greatest cause for concern as they can devastate whole plantations. In the tourist areas, the buildings weaken the power of the wind and the coastal areas fare better as a result. Salvation usually comes to man and nature after three to five days, in the form of heavy rain that chases the strong winds away.

The cultural scene

Tenerife may well be an isolated island, but that is no reason to assume that the islanders are cut off from world culture. Quite the reverse is true, as any visitor will see from the wide selection of books available in the bookshops in the college town of La Laguna, or in Santa Cruz and Puerto de la Cruz. It is impossible to overlook the fact that practically all the important writers in the world whose works have been translated into Spanish are represented here. Anyone with a passing knowledge of Spanish can glance through the daily newspaper and find that a variety of courses, seminars and lectures are offered. If you wish to learn something of the language and culture while you're here, you won't have much difficulty in finding a Spanish course for tourists. There is a popular saying which maintains that *Canarias es tierra de poetas,* 'The Canaries is a land of poets'. The beauty of the landscape, together with the inherent desire to discover wider horizons, has produced many a poet – Pedro García Cabura, Marcel Ríos Ruiz and Julio Tovar are among the most highly acclaimed. The inhabitants of Tenerife have wide and varied intellectual and artistic interests. The lively cultural scene on the island provides evidence of this. Many concerts, theatre and operatic performances are staged in the main towns. Unfortunately, visitors to the island who cannot understand Spanish will have to make do with the musical events.

Agriculture

Even on Tenerife, young people are choosing to leave their villages and are heading for the tourist centres and the main towns in search of employment, allowing acres of fertile land to fall into the hands of speculators. Nevertheless, agriculture still plays an important part in the island's economy and social structure. The agricultural history of Tenerife serves as a warning to many of today's farmers that one-crop farming often leads to disaster. In the past, international factors have contributed to crises in the cultivation of sugar cane, vines, prickly pear (for breeding the cochineal, an insect used to produce red dye) and bananas. Recently, the island's farmers have switched to more diversified crops, making bananas, tomatoes, oranges, potatoes, avocado pears, grapes, strawberries and flowers today's mainstays of the agricultural industry. Banana cultivation is still predominant, but given the rising production costs and the strong Central American competition, trade in this fruit has suffered. The plantations are found mainly in the lower-lying regions along the north coast and in the south-west. Cultivating banana trees requires much careful work, as the soil needs to be tended and plenty of water is essential — it takes between 16 and 19 months before the tree bears fruit. About 95% of Tenerife's banana crop goes to mainland Spain. Elsewhere on the island, the steep hillsides have been terraced to assist crop cultivation. Nevertheless, soil erosion, a rocky sub-soil, water shortages and the baking sun make for back-breaking work. It is often impossible to bring tractors onto the slopes and a proper, extensive irrigation system is required. In the arid south, farmers still use the Canarian dry-field cultivation system. The soil is covered with porous, water-retaining basalt granules, which at night absorb water from the moist soil, thereby helping to prevent evaporation and erosion. Alongside bananas, goats' cheese and a robust red wine are two other home-grown products that play a significant part in the island's economy. Chickens, rabbits and pigs are bred to meet the local demand for meat, while flowers have become a lucrative export product. The bird-of-paradise flower *(Strelitzia reginae)* is a popular souvenir for tourists.

Lucha canaria

Canarian wrestling is a very popular sport amongst the locals, and some contests are even broadcast on regional television. This sport probably originated in a contest played out by the Guanches. Unlike conventional wrestling, it is not a game for two, rather it's a team sport with 12 players on each side, and each team represents a district, village or island. Each wrestler is garbed in a shirt and a pair of trousers made from coarse linen. The trouser-legs, which are rolled up as high as possible on the thighs, play an important part of the game: opponents may grasp only this item of clothing and the player who manages to knock over an opponent within the ring wins a point. Anyone watching a contest for the first time might easily get the (mistaken) impression that the game consists of 24 athletes trying to pull each other's trousers off! Anyhow, Canarian wrestling requires great physical strength and quick reflexes. As with judo, the status of the wrestler is apparent from the colour of his belt. Beginners wear white belts, followed by yellow, orange, green, black, red and blue.

Flora

The great German naturalist and explorer Alexander von Humboldt said that Tenerife was blessed with a magnificent flora characteristic of tropical latitudes, and he was right: over 2,000 different plant species grow on the Canaries, but only 700 are unique to Tenerife. Given the various climatic zones on the steep mountains, the vegetation can be divided into five categories according to the elevation of the land. Tropical and sub-tropical plants thrive below

TENERIFE IN CONTEXT

600 m (2,000 feet) above sea level, and extensive banana plantations cover the lower slopes of the northern side. Eucalyptus trees, Canarian cedars, planes, mimosas, palisanders, rubber trees, blue-flowering jacaranda trees and various types of palm and laurel border the gardens, streets and squares. Hibiscus, bougainvillaea, tulip and orchid trees flower practically all year round, while giant-sized poinsettias grow like weeds. Roses of every colour, lilies, white calla lilies and the orange-flowering bird-of-paradise adorn many gardens. Cacti and agaves (century plants) grow in the south, up to an altitude of 1,000 m (3,500 feet). Between 600 and 1,500 m (2,000 and 5,000 feet), fields of potatoes and cabbages are separated by chestnuts and eucalyptus groves. In the Anaga mountains, laurel woods with ferns, hollies and tree heath form a dense 'primeval forest'. Above 1,500 m (5,000 feet), wide expanses of pine forest provide shelter for broom, heather, mushrooms and a number of plants unique to the Canary Islands. Above 2,000 m (6,500 feet), the endemic, exclusive Canarian varieties grow, eleven of which are found only in the Cañadas and on the Teide. One highly unusual species found only here is the dragon tree. It has hard, pointed leaves around a fan-shaped crown supported by a tall, rough trunk. It is a member of the lily family and can grow to a height of 20 m (65 feet). One especially grand example, now an essential part of the tourist sights, is the dragon tree at Icod de los Vinos. It is estimated to be from 400 to 3,000 years old. Lacking annual rings, its age can only be inferred from the number of branches – not an easy task, as new ones appear at regular intervals. If you scratch the bark, the oozing resin turns blood red. The Guanches used this 'dragon's blood' to embalm their dead.

Fauna
Tenerife's fauna is significantly less varied than its flora. There are only four species of mammalian wildlife: rabbits, mouflons (wild sheep introduced in the 1970s by hunters), bats and hedgehogs. As far as reptiles are concerned, they are represented by two groups: lizards and skinks. One species of lizard, dark with greenish markings on its back, is endemic. The small gecko, with small suction pads on its toes, can often be seen clinging to ceilings and is regarded by the locals as a harbinger of good luck. The skink, a small, smooth-skinned lizard, has an olive-green back with black sides. Small, light-green tree frogs are often heard croaking in the evenings. Beetles, cockroaches and butterflies represent the insect world; beautifully coloured butterflies, some with wing spans of up to 10 cm (4 inches), can be seen flitting from blossom to blossom. There are several species of spider, but no scorpions or poisonous snakes exist on Tenerife. However, the noxious mosquitoes are alive and well. A wide variety of bird species thrives on the Canary Islands; some congregating only in the west-

ern islands, and others are confined to only one island. The blue Teide finch, one species of woodpecker *(picapinos)* and one species of robin breed only on Tenerife. Other indigenous birds include the peregrine falcon, the golden eagle, the wild pigeon, the raven and the most famous Canarian bird, the rather unspectacular Canarian finch, from which the bright yellow cage bird, the Canary bird, was bred. Some migratory birds winter on the island. Tenerife's waters abound with fish. *Viejas*, types of mullet that vary in colour from pink to silver grey, *salemas, chicharros*, sardines, *merluza* (hake), tuna, morays and many others can be seen displayed on the fishmongers' slabs. A large selection of squid *(calamares)*, octopus *(pulpos)* and shellfish, such as mussels *(mejillones)* and, of course, prawns and lobsters.

Tinerfeños

Tenerife's local population is mostly comprised of farming and fishing families, who have been hard hit by unemployment in recent years. State education was badly neglected under Franco; it was only in the 1970s, with the country's democratization, that compulsory education was taken seriously. The local language is a Spanish dialect resembling Latin American Spanish; particularly noticeable is the dropping of the letter 's' and word endings that are not fully articulated. The *Tinerfeños* jokingly describe themselves as *chicharreros*, after the *chicharro* fish. It is generally true that the islanders are a proud people, and they place a high value on appearances and on giving a good impression to outsiders. Mediterranean in spirit, they are warm-hearted and vivacious, though certain Latin clichés do prevail. Machismo still reigns supreme amongst men, and gossip is the favourite pastime of many women. Tourism, however, has precipitated the emancipation of women, who now participate fully in running the community, notably being employed in the tourism and public administration sectors. In fact, the majority of the students attending La Laguna University are women.

Young people delight in making noise – the louder and the higher-pitched the noise of their mopeds, the better. During the many fiestas, the music volume is set to high, and the music carries on until the early morning hours – as do the firecrackers, fireworks and gun salutes. Some outsiders who know the people well complain that the *Tinerfeños* are selfish and live only for the moment, and that their charm is just a cover for their insecurity. Tourists usually see only the helpful and friendly side, but it is inadvisable to demand too much from them, as visitors may find themselves cold-shouldered. Nevertheless, the locals do have a sense of humour, and they laugh and sing a lot. In contrast, they take their Catholic faith very seriously.

Handicrafts

For many village families, handmade items are the only source of income. Standing on the out-

TENERIFE IN CONTEXT

side, it can be difficult to identify small family-run businesses, but you only need to peek through the windows and doors of these old houses. Goods are often made for the larger companies that supply the tourist shops with these rustic products. Typical handmade goods include table cloths or materials edged with the traditional Canarian hemstitch, crochetwork, musical instruments, knives with ornate handles, embroidery, pottery and engraved jewellery. Often the goods not bought by the wholesaler are sold directly to the tourists by the craftsmen themselves. In the remote rural areas, it is quite common to find women selling their modest wares from roadside stands. To haggle over prices in these circumstances would not really be fair. Many of these home-based artisans gather together at the *ferias*, a sort of craft fair, and sell the fruits of their labours directly to the tourists. Every area on the island has its speciality. La Orotava, Los Realejos, La Guancha, San Juan de la Rambla and Granadilla are noted for their *calados*, hemstitch embroidery. Tablecloths, place mats and napkins, as well as blouses are often decorated with this characteristic needlework. In La Guancha and the area around Buenavista and Masca, woven baskets and straw hats are produced. A straw cord is wrapped with soft thread, wool, raffia or hemp. The cord is then wound into a spiral and sewn together. Companies in La Orotava and Los Realejos specialize in making large baskets for shops. Bird cages made from bamboo canes are found in San Andrés and Icod de los Vinos, as is traditional pottery made in the Guanche style (i.e., not with a potter's wheel), including vases, ashtrays and jewellery boxes. Pottery studios are found in Los Cristianos, La Orotava and Güímar. The *Canarios* are skilled woodcarvers and the furniture craftsmen of Buenavista, La Orotava and La Laguna in particular enjoy a good reputation. Musical instruments, such as the four-stringed *timple* (a small guitar), are made in Taganana and San Andrés. Locals also create handsome plates, cutlery, garlic mortars and cheese slices carved out of wood. Traditional Canarian wine presses and mini-balconies are produced in La Orotava and Los Realejos.

Water resources

In order to reach the watertable and the island's precious water reserves, it has been necessary to cut kilometre-long shafts or *galerías* into the mountainsides. There are now over 1,000 such shafts with only about 200 yielding any water. The extracted water is then channelled to the villages and then pumped to the banana plantations. The right to draw water is largely in the hands of private landowners who, in some cases, date their ancestry back to the Spanish conquest, when the land was apportioned amongst them. Water reserves are also stored in the *presas*, large open basins into which rainwater and excess water from the *galerías* flow.

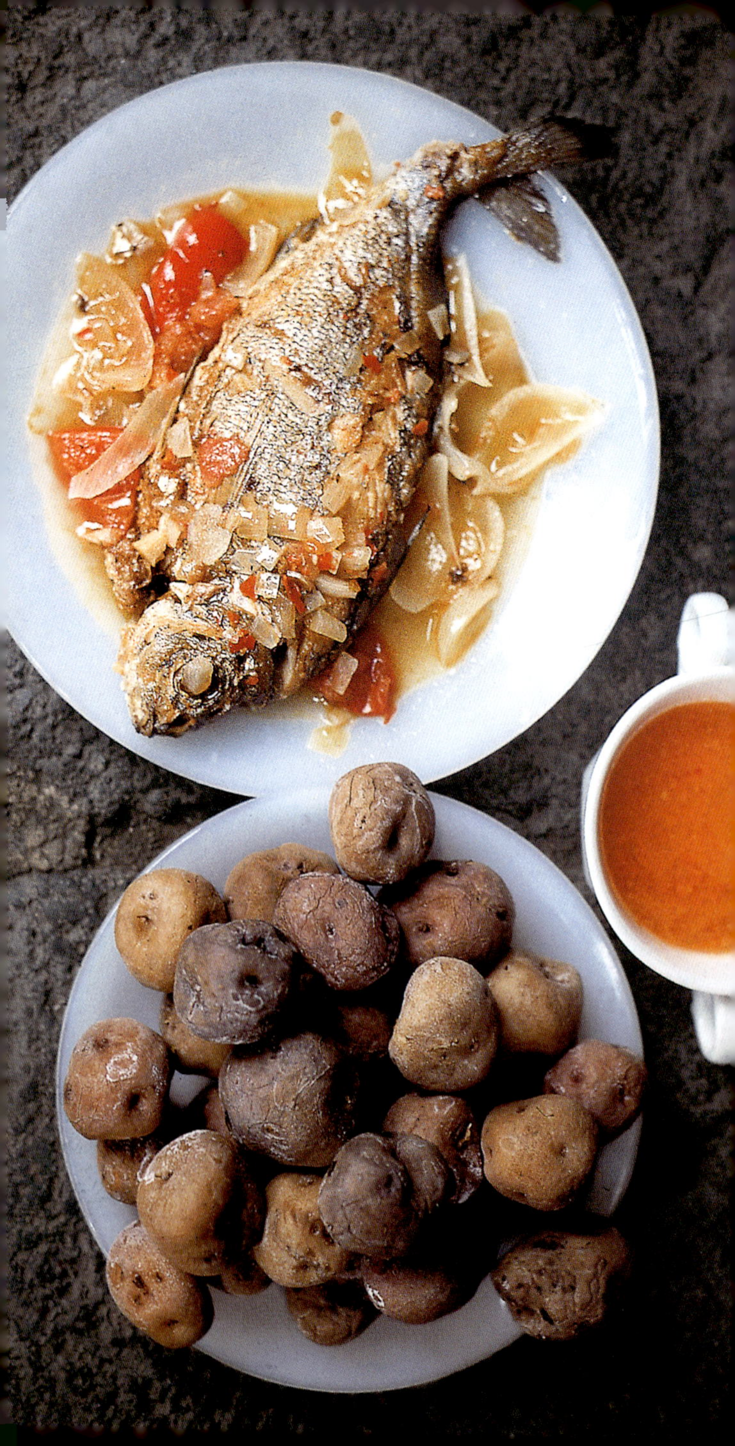

FOOD & DRINK

Canarian cuisine

Hearty stews, home-grown vegetables and plenty of delicious fresh fish make for simple, yet very tasty local fare

Good, hearty food is fundamental to the Canarian way of life and *Tinerfeños* certainly know how to eat well. The local cuisine is simple and down-to-earth, both in preparation and in presentation, and is made from plenty of fresh, home-grown ingredients that guarantee flavourful results. Canarians don't believe in ceremony at the dinner table and those who are accustomed to swish foyers, expensive cutlery and liveried waiters will need to adjust to a different environment. The scene that unfolds behind a great portal may not be quite as grand as you had anticipated; on the other hand, a simple façade may conceal some very pleasant surprises.

Some of the best eateries are tucked away in the rural and coastal villages, where bars and restaurants are often little more than converted garages that could easily be overlooked by passing tourists. Of course, the main resorts and large towns cater to a more international clientele, where it is possible to dine in a more European style. If you cannot survive without a full English breakfast and Yorkshire pudding at lunchtime, suitable restaurants abound. There are even a number of Chinese restaurants to satisfy cravings for prawns and chow mein. But if you want to sample authentic Canarian cuisine, you need to venture beyond the boundaries of the tourist resorts.

A visit to a typical Canarian restaurant often proves to be more than just a culinary experience. Guests are generally seated in an open patio, surrounded by greenery and flowers, with perhaps a gently splashing fountain amongst them. The ceilings within are supported by thick, solid beams and the walls are used to display trinkets and old-fashioned cooking utensils. This is the classic type of restaurant you'll come across in Puerto de la Cruz and the inland villages. However, such establishments don't necessarily serve genuine Canarian food, so the best way to find the real thing is to follow your nose. If you can detect the

A traditionally prepared Canarian fish dish, served with salt-encrusted 'papas arrugadas'

waft of braised meat, fish, herbs and, of course, garlic, then you are on the right track. Such mouth-watering smells emanate from guaranteed palate-pleasers, conjured up from the island's staple fare: fish and seafood, chicken, rabbit, potatoes and many fresh vegetables.

The classic starter is always soup *(sopa)* – vegetable soup *(sopa de verdura)* or fish soup *(sopa de pescado)*, prepared with many kinds of seafood. Garlic soup *(sopa de ajo)* is well worth a try. A Canarian speciality are the *papas arrugadas*, served practically always as a side dish. These small, wrinkled potatoes are served in a covered pot, having been steamed either in seawater or in liberally salted tapwater until all the liquid has evaporated, leaving a crusted layer of dried salt over the potato skins, which may be either eaten or discarded.

If you want to eat like a *Canario*, there's no escape from garlic, the fundamental ingredient of local cuisine. Liberally added to meat and fish dishes, soups and especially to the hot *mojo* sauces that accompany most specialities. To prepare the red sauce *(mojo rojo)*, sea salt, hot paprika or chilies and garlic are crushed with a pestle and mortar, then mixed together thoroughly with vinegar and oil. It tastes a bit like a spicy vinaigrette. The *mojo verde* is a green variation, for which coriander or parsley is used instead of paprika.

During inland excursions, it is not unusual to hear the sound of gunshots from the hunters' rifles; they are not firing at lost dogs or cats, but instead at the prolific wild rabbits *(conejos salvajes)*. In most tourist areas, however, the rabbit served in restaurants is domestically reared rather than wild. These *conejos mansos* are especially bred for the plate. The most popular rabbit dish is rabbit in hot sauce, *conejo salmorejo,* with *papas arrugadas* and *patatas fritas* (chips) or *patatas sorpresa* (surprise potatoes).

Chicken is another favourite that is usually served from the spit, though it also comes braised. A tasty Canarian speciality is diced chicken that has been braised in a hot, rather oily sauce, and is served with *papas*. Another typical local dish is the stew called *puchero*, made with pieces of meat, potatoes and vegetables. If it has chick peas and noodles instead then it is called *rancho.*

By far the most popular types of fish are the sea bass, the hake and the parrot-fish, *cherne, merluza,* and *vieja*, respectively. Sole is often featured on menus, but it is usually imported frozen from more remote fishing grounds. If you really want well-prepared sole, it is better to seek out a high-quality fish restaurant, as proper preparation is often skimped in the simpler establishments. On the other hand, shellfish caught in local waters is treated as a real delicacy, one that is greatly appreciated by the islanders themselves, who are experts in its preparation. Gourmets will relish the king prawns *(langostinos)*, prawns *(gambas)*, crabs *(cangrejos)* and various types of mussel and whelk *(lapas)*. The small varieties of octopus *(pulpos)* are sliced into pieces, fried and

FOOD & DRINK

served as *tapas*. Squid *(calamar)* is served whole or chopped into morsels also as a *tapa*.

Banana-based desserts are a common menu item. A favourite is flambéd banana sweetened with a liqueur and honey, although crème caramel and almond tart *(tocino de cielo, tarta de almendras)* are also popular choices.

Tapas

Tapas are neither hors d'oeuvres nor the main course, but several portions of them can add up to a main dish. Usually, they are small plates filled with pieces of crispy sausage or meatballs in sauce, little herring fillets or tuna salad with spicy seasoning. Another favourite is potato salad with finely chopped eggs and fresh herbs. Most locals savour *tapas* as a mid-morning snack to fill the gap between breakfast and what many would regard as a late lunch, but often it's just a good excuse to disappear into a bar for a drink!

Cheese

Although Tenerife does not boast many well-known cheeses, such as those produced on the neighbouring islands of La Palma and Hierro, the *Tinerfeños* are real cheese fanatics. The white goats' cheese, *queso blanco*, is one local cheese, but there are plenty of other good Canarian cheeses, including a superbly flavoured smoked goats' cheese.

Wines

One hundred ears ago, wine was one of Tenerife's main exports. Today, although production has tapered off, the quality has improved dramatically as small wine producers have invested in modern equipment to process the grape juice. Until recently, wine was sold in bars as basic table wine, but many cellars now supply it in bottles endorsed with a quality seal. The vintages of Tenerife have received numerous awards, with the reds from Tacoronte and the whites from Icod/La Guancha at the forefront. Red wines are produced mainly around Santa Ursula, La Victoria, Tacoronte and La Matanza. White and rosé wines are predominantly from Icod de los Vinos, Los Realejos and La Guancha. Nevertheless, the local production is unable to meet the demand of the many restaurants and hotels, so wines from the European mainland, primarily from Spain, must be imported.

Other beverages

After breakfast, a rather modest meal by northern European standards, the bars fill up quickly. The most likely choice for the locals will be a *cortado*, an espresso with condensed milk, or else a glass of red wine. Mineral water bottled at Vilaflor and in the Orotava valley helps to quench your thirst after exertions in the hot sun. *Cogñac*, officially described as brandy, is also popular and there is a wide choice of brands and flavours. Wine is consumed in large quantities at any time of the day, and you can get cold beer on tap in most places. Bars in the tourist resorts sell English, Dutch and German beers. In the evenings, many restaurants offer the famous *sangría*, a type of punch

What's on the menu?

beer:	*cerveza*	ice-cream:	*helado*
the bill:	*la cuenta*	knife:	*cuchillo*
bread:	*pan*	meat:	*carne*
butter:	*mantequilla*	menu:	*lista, menú*
cheese:	*queso*	omelette:	*tortilla*
chips:	*patatas fritas*	rice:	*arroz*
dessert:	*postre*	salad:	*ensalada*
dish:	*plato*	steak:	*filete*
fish:	*pescado*	vegetables:	*legumbres*
fork:	*tenedor*	waiter:	*camarero*
glass:	*vaso*	water:	*aqua*
ham:	*jamón*	wine:	*vino*

based on red wine but mixed with other, stronger spirits — watch out, it is often deceptively strong. When it comes to coffee, order a *café solo* (espresso) or a *cortado,* maybe also a *carajillo* (espresso with *cogñac*). If you like filtered coffee, then you should order *café alemán* ('German coffee').

Gofio

What flour is to the northern Europeans, *gofio* is to Canarians, although the natives accord it a much higher status. It is believed that the Guanches discovered this staple food, which is made from roasted barley, wheat or maize flour. It continues to be an important component of the local diet. Called *gofio* — meaning the 'bread of the poor' by the Spanish conquistadors, it has no place on restaurant menus, although it is a very important item in the domestic larder. Many agricultural workers and shepherds still eat *gofio* to keep them going during the day. They carry a leather pouch *(zurrón)* made from goatskin, in which the *gofio* is prepared as required: flour is mixed with milk or water and, once it is well kneaded, bite-sized chunks are pulled from the dough and eaten. It may not be everyone's favourite daytime snack, but it's one that is greatly appreciated by the local farm workers.

Mealtimes

In marked contrast to the northern European, the *Tinerfeño* eats very late; lunch *(almuerzo)* is rarely eaten before 2 pm and families don't usually gather for the evening meal *(cena)* before 8 or 9 pm. To bridge the gap, it's not unusual to have a late afternoon snack *(merienda)*, usually a sandwich. For many Canarians, eating is an extended ritual especially on the weekends when the village restaurants fill up and the occasion is usually a lively one. Everyone enjoys it, and the noisy chatter continues until late. Bones accumulate on the table and left-overs are fed to the dogs. Some people turn up their noses at the apparent lack of hygiene but, for Canarians, if a meal is to be fully appreciated,

FOOD & DRINK

there must be plenty of food to go around.

Breakfast *(desayuno)* is fairly standard and simple, consisting mainly of coffee with milk *(café con leche)* or a small, strong espresso, taken either black *(café solo)* or with a dash of milk *(café cortado)*, a sandwich or bocadillo, a white roll with a sweet filling, such as jam or honey, or a thick wedge of ham, cheese or chorizo, the much-loved Spanish spicy sausage.

In many of the restaurants along the coast, guests are invited to select their own fish directly from the kitchen, the price is then determined by weight. Side dishes, such as potatoes and salads, are charged separately. An adopted habit is to put bread and butter on the table before the main course arrives; the cost of this starter (usually between 25p and 75p) is then added to the bill, whether it is eaten or not. If you don't want this additional item, then you should hand it back as soon as it is put on the table.

Restaurant categories

There are various categories of restaurant on Tenerife, but the official classification that uses a scale of forks (1-5) is rather arbitrary as it doesn't seem to reflect the quality of the food or service very accurately. Most restaurants are described as *Bar/Restaurante* and are a combination of restaurant, wine bar and pub. They offer both à la carte and set menus. Away from the tourist resorts, many establishments describe themselves simply as a *Bar*, although they often serve full meals. *Bodegas* are the real wine bars, often in a cellar-style setting. Many villages have corner shops or *ventas* that double as bars. The prices here are surprisingly low.

Open-air dining under the laurels in Adeje

Verde

HANDICRAFT
ARTESANIA CANARIA

SHOPPING & SOUVENIRS

Woodcarvers and lacemakers

Markets in the towns and villages regale the senses with colourful sights and mouth-watering smells

Take a quick stroll down the main shopping street on arrival and it will be apparent after only a few glances that Tenerife has plenty to offer to the dedicated shopper. Pedestrian zones and shopping malls are crammed with boutiques, and the ambiance is not unlike that of an Eastern bazaar. Many of the shops are run by industrious Indians; the shelves are piled high with goods from all over the world, including all kinds of electronic household goods. Electric razors and other household appliances are sold at bargain prices. Jewellery shop windows gleam with jade and ivory, semi-precious stones and sparkling rings, pearls and gold and silver chains. An amazing variety of junky souvenirs and bric-a-brac of questionable value overflow from the bargain boxes placed at the shops' entrances to draw the customers in. If you like Oriental-style shopping and want to haggle, the traders will be happy to oblige.

Souvenirs for all tastes can be found in Los Cristianos

If you are looking for quality and authenticity, however, then it is better to seek out the specialist shops, where usually English is spoken. When buying jewellery, clocks or photographic equipment, don't be tempted by the suspiciously low prices: the quality is nearly always reflected in the price.

Nowadays, it is virtually impossible to find and buy genuine antiques, even though you may see plenty that capture your attention. The objects on sale are likely to be new, but given an 'antique' finish.

There are many offerings for lovers of modern art, who stand a good chance of picking up a memorable keepsake from one of the many art galleries and shops that sell oil paintings, prints and reproductions.

A number of resorts boast modern multi-storeyed shopping centres. These labyrinthine complexes house everything from luxury boutiques selling the latest fashions to high-class jewellers and accessory shops to bazaars, bars, cafés and restaurants. The atmosphere in these consumer havens hovers between that of a supermarket, a games hall and a dealing room. Customers rummage, fumble and snatch until they fall upon the perfect outfit for the beach or nightclub. Around the corner, teenagers try on unlabelled jeans at rock-bottom prices. The innumerable scents of perfume and cosmetics are hard to resist, especially as the well-known brands are readily available and the prices rarely matched even by the duty-free shops at the airport. *Rebajas* are end-of-season sales, and a sign saying *liquidación total* indicates a closing-down sale; both are well worth looking into. Many shops claim to have year-round *rebajas*, but those supposedly rock-bottom prices are in reality discounts from raised prices. When it comes to alcohol and cigarettes, though, these are remarkably cheap indeed, especially in the supermarkets.

Leather goods from Spain or Africa are popular souvenirs, while handmade products from the Canary Islands in general and Tenerife in particular make more conventional souvenirs. Tenerife is renowned for its craft industry. Pottery, woodcarvings and straw or cane basketware are skilfully and painstakingly produced by craftsmen, either in their own homes or in small workshops. Canarian embroidery, especially the open threadwork pieces from Tenerife, is of outstanding quality. With this type of sewing, the material is partially unravelled and then, with a special hemstitching technique, patterns and motifs such as suns and roses are stitched on. The production of these filigree patterns has be-

Tenerife lace in the making

come a real art form on the island and the observant visitor will spot a variety of motifs embroidered on tablecloths, place mats and handkerchiefs. The lace from Vilaflor and La Palma, which has been made by the same family for more than 50 years, is reputed to be among the best. Sadly, this is a dying art as fewer and fewer women are carrying on the tradition.

To truly indulge all the senses, a visit to at least one of the outdoor markets is a must. Everything that nature has bestowed on the island in such abundance is displayed here in all its colourful glory. Traders peddle their wares, competing for customers with booming voices. Fruit, vegetables, flowers and house plants spill over heavily laden stalls. The scent of Oriental spices, the smell of fish stalls and the musty odour of fresh seaweed combine with the earthy pungency of live chickens, rabbits and ducks to create an aromatic blend that rewards passers-by (provided they can overcome their inhibitions) with a veritable symphony for the nose.

EVENTS

Carpets of flowers

With festivals and carnivals all year round, the inhabitants of Tenerife certainly know how to celebrate

The following days are public holidays, when banks, offices and post offices close. However, many towns have their own individual festivals, usually the patron saint's day, in which case local closures will apply.

PUBLIC HOLIDAYS & FESTIVALS

January
1 January: *Año Nuevo*, New Year's Day
6 January: *Los Reyes Magos*, Epiphany, when children are given presents; on the previous day, the three kings parade through town.
22 January: *Fiesta de San Sebastián*, the feast of St Sebastian, the patron saint of Garachico and Los Realejos
Early January to mid-February: ★ *Canary Island Music Festival*; classical music in Santa Cruz and La Orotava.

February
2 February: *Candelaria*, Candlemas; patronal festival in Candelaria
February/March: ★ *Carnival*. Processions, flamboyant costumes, music and dancing in the streets and squares throughout the island. The highlights are the crowning of the carnival queen in Santa Cruz and the 'Burial of the Sardine'.

March/April
2 March: *Fiesta de San Benito Abad*, Feast of St Benedict in La Laguna
March/April: *Semana Santa*, Holy Week. All the holy statues are taken from inside the churches and paraded through the streets. Especially impressive are the ★ Holy Week processions in Santa Cruz and La Laguna.
March/April: *Pascua*, Easter

May/June
1 May: *Día del Trabajo*, Labour Day; beginning of the May festivals. Flower display in Santa Cruz
3 May: *Día de la Cruz*, Feast of the Cross, holidays in all places bearing the name 'Cruz'. Religious processions in which locals carry a cross. All over the island, crosses are decorated with flowers and firework displays are held.
May/June: *Pentecostés*, Whitsun
May/June: *Corpus Christi*. Solemn processions throughout the island. La Orotava and La Laguna are the best places to see the ★ ornate pavement tableaux designed with freshly cut flowers
30 May: *Día de Canarias*, Canary Island Day

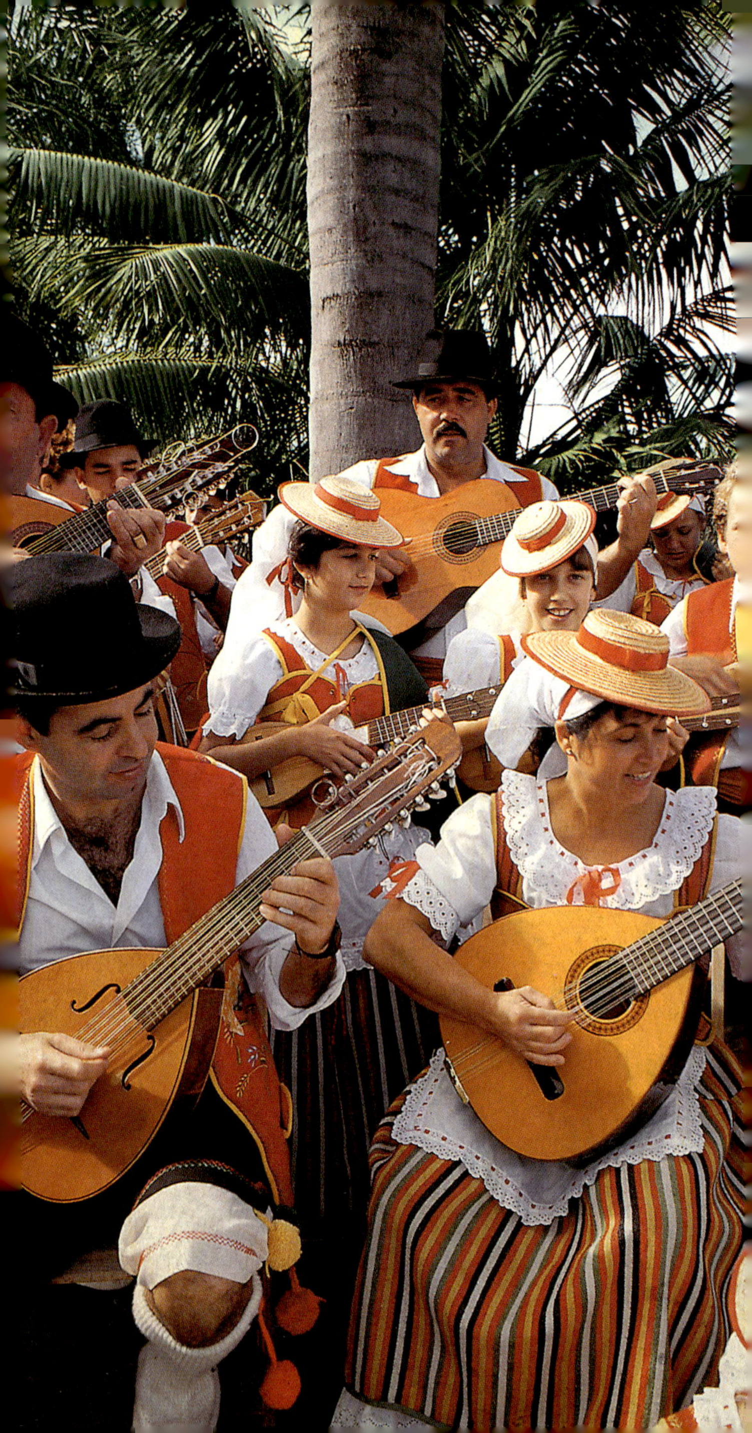

EVENTS

June/July
3rd Sunday after Whitsun: ★ *Romería de San Isidro*; revellers in La Orotava parade through the streets in brightly coloured costumes.
1st Sunday in July: *Fiesta y Romería de San Benito Abad*, Feast of St Benedict and pilgrimage in La Laguna
16 July: ★*Fiesta de la Virgen del Carmen y del Gran Poder* in Puerto de la Cruz. Feast of the patron saint with procession of fishing boats off the coast. The festivities, centred in the old town and the Plaza del Charco, last almost all of July.
25 July: *Fiesta de Santiago Apóstol*, Feast of St James, the patron saint of Spain

August
15 August: *Asunción de María*, Assumption. ★ *Romería de la Virgen de Candelaria*; pilgrims from all over the island come to Candelaria to honour the patroness of the archipelago
3rd Sunday in August: *Fiesta de Cristo del Gran Poder* in Bajamar

September
7–21 September: *Fiesta del Santísimo* in La Laguna and Tacoronte

October
5 October: *Fiesta de la Misericordia* in Garachico
12 October: *Día de la Hispanidad* (Day of the Discovery of the Americas, a national holiday), *Fiesta de Nuestra Señora del Pilar*

December
6 December: *Día de la Constitución*, Day of the Constitution, a national holiday
8 December: *Inmaculada Concepción*, Immaculate Conception
25 December: *Navidad del Señor*, Christmas Day

A folk group in traditional costume plays traditional Tenerife music

---

MARCO POLO SELECTION: EVENTS

1 Carnival
Spectacular carnival festivities in every town and village (page 31)

2 Semana Santa
Grand carnival processions in Santa Cruz and La Laguna (page 31)

3 Corpus Christi
Ornate flower carpets celebrating Corpus Christi in La Orotava and La Laguna (page 31)

4 Romería de San Isidro
Harvest thanksgiving in La Orotava (page 33)

5 Fiestas de Julio
Procession of boats in Puerto de la Cruz (page 33)

6 Romería de la Virgen de Candelaria
Festival of the Virgin Mary lasting several days (page 33)

7 Canary Island Music Festival
Classical music in Santa Cruz and La Orotava (page 31)

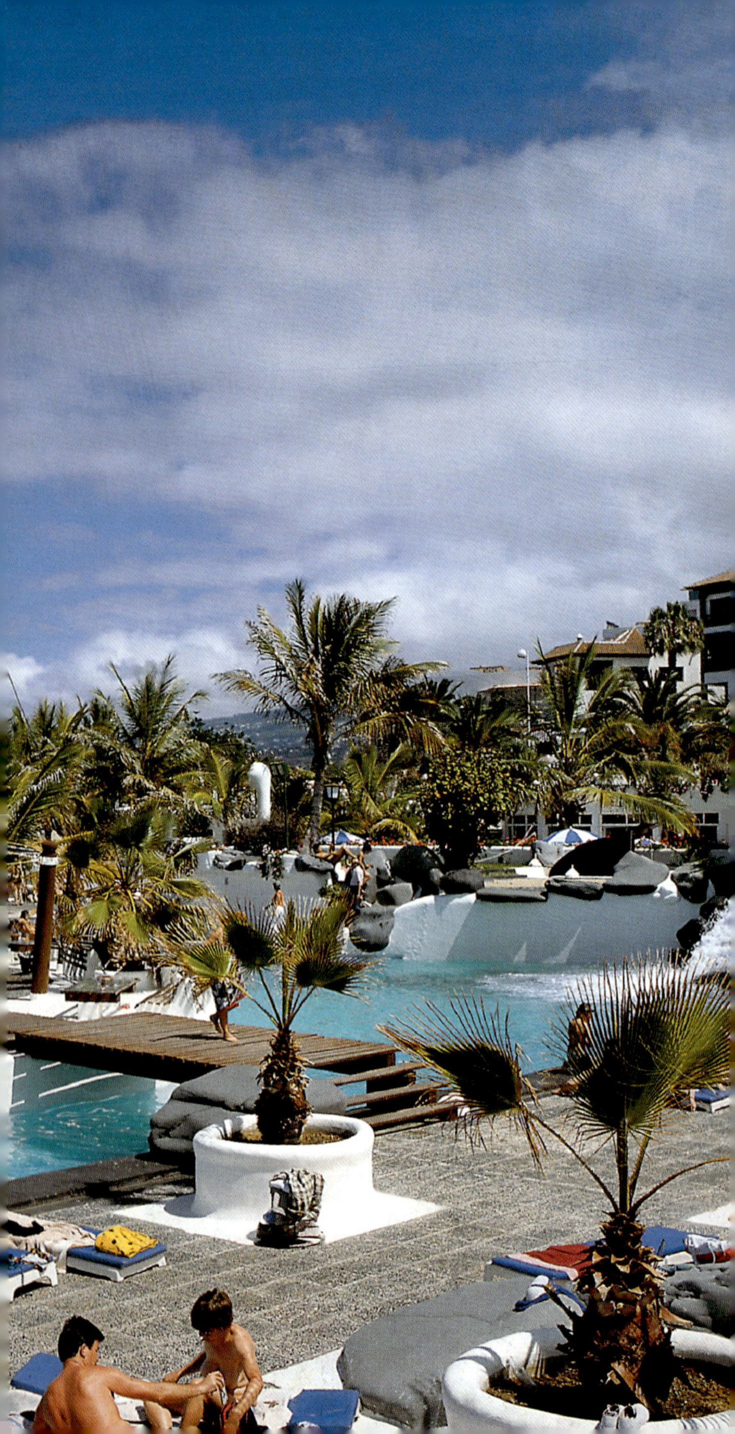

THE NORTH-WEST COAST

Paradise on earth

Historic towns and charming fishing villages nestle amongst banana plantations and vineyards

The stretch of motorway that hugs the coastline along the 5-km (3-miles)-wide Orotava valley is quite breathtaking, offering beautiful views of the sea beyond a steep and sloping verdant landscape. Banana plantations are everywhere, interspersed with the occasional palm tree, brightly coloured flowers and gleaming white villages.

Public sea-water swimming pools in Puerto de la Cruz

Standing guard over it all is the mighty Teide, with its bright, cone-shaped peak. Towering hotel blocks line the lower coastal stretch beside Puerto de la Cruz. The 100-m (330-foot)-high Tigaiga precipice rises out of the western end of the valley; beyond, a sheer rocky ridge extends as far as Garachico. The lower region is barren and rocky, while the higher is more fertile land worked by the locals. Pine forests and terraced fields, where pota-

---

Hotel and restaurant prices

Hotels

Category 1: 20,000-25,000 ptas
Category 2: 13,500-20,000 ptas
Category 3: under 13,500 ptas
These prices are for two persons in a double room, breakfast included. Hotels have up to four different seasonal price categories.

Restaurants

Category 1: 2,000-2,500 ptas
Category 2: 1,100-2,000 ptas
Category 3: 950-1,100 ptas
Prices are per person for a main dish, beverages excluded.

Important abbreviations

Avda.	*Avenida*	Avenue
C/.	*Calle*	Street
Ctra.	*Carretera*	Main road
Edf.	*Edificio*	Building
ptas	*Pesetas*	Pesetas
Urb.	*Urbanización*	(Holiday-) village

toes and vines are cultivated, characterize the sloping landscape. The Isla Baja beyond Guarachico is much flatter, and oranges and bananas are grown here. To the south of the Isla Baja, the steep Teno hills rise up and continue on toward the sea behind Buenavista. At the western tip, Punta de Teno is ringed by a small, isolated plain and from here it's a tortuous route southward across the 1,000-m (3,300-foot)-high Teno hills, cut through by deep gorges and steep precipices. Small, impoverished villages nestle in the valleys, surrounded by leafy vegetation. Forests of laurels and tree heaths alternate with cultivated strips and palm tree groves.

LA OROTAVA

(106/C2) Sturdy shoes and a strong pair of legs are required for the steep streets of this picturesque town of 36,000 inhabitants. Cobble stone roads wind their way along the sheer slopes of the Orotava valley. Old churches, monasteries and palaces testify to the wealth that the fertile valley bestowed on the Spanish colonists. Many of the houses, with their ornately carved shutters, balconies and oriel windows, date from the 17th and 18th centuries.

La Orotava is divided by the gorge Barranco Araujo, separating the houses on its way towards the valley. In the middle of the town lies the Plaza de la Constitución, which crosses the Barranco Araujo on a two-level platform. This square is sometimes referred to as the 'balcony of La Orotava' because of the stunning panorama it offers over the rooftops and right across to the sea. To the northeast of the square stands the church and former cloister of San Agustín, now barracks. Founded during the early 16th century, the town quickly became an influential and prosperous settlement. Today, La Orotava remains an important business, administrative and educational centre that is largely untouched by the advent of tourism.

SIGHTS

Botanical Garden
This small park lies behind the town hall, and is an annex of the renowned botanical garden situated between Puerto de la Cruz and La Orotava. Here you will find many plants from Australia, Malaysia, India and South America.

Casas de los Balcones
★ Of all the balcony houses on the Calle San Francisco, distinguished by their beautifully sculpted verandas and inner courtyards, No. 4 stands out. This grand mansion dates back to the mid-17th century and now houses a school for embroidery. Handmade crafts and other souvenirs are made here. *C/. San Francisco*

Convento Molina
Crafts, pictures and other gifts and souvenirs are for sale in this old convent from 1590. The flower-carpeted balcony offers a fine view of the valley. *C/. San Francisco*

THE NORTH-WEST COAST

Gofio mill
The unique *gofio* is still milled here. One room is reserved for roasting the barley, another one for grinding it. Old photographs displayed on the walls show how the mill functioned in the days before electricity, when the wheel was turned by a stream flowing through the street (in which the women did their washing). The remains of two other abandoned mills can be seen higher up the steep street. *C/. Dr Domingo González*

Church of Nuestra Señora de la Concepción
★ The island's finest Baroque church dates from the 18th century. A large, self-supporting dome with a smaller dome on top gives the illusion of a high nave. The statues of the Mater Dolorosa and of St John by Luján Pérez can be seen in the side altars. The central marble altar and the pulpit were done by Italian artists. *Plaza Casañas*

Liceo de Taoro
This idyllic castle is used as a theatre, for locally sponsored cultural events. *Plaza de la Constitución*

Museo Ibero-americano
The former Dominican monastery of Santo Domingo, located

MARCO POLO SELECTION: THE NORTH-WEST COAST

1 Aguamansa
Popular walking area amid pine forests at 1,000 m (3,300 feet) above sea level (page 45)

2 Casas de los Balcones
A typical Canarian balcony house in La Orotava's Calle San Francisco; now home to an embroidery school (page 36)

3 Playa Jardín
The new 'garden' beach in Puerto de la Cruz, designed by the brilliant architect César Manrique (page 44)

4 Dragon tree
The island's landmark in Icod de los Vinos (page 47)

5 Nuestra Señora de la Concepción
An interesting church in La Orotava (page 37)

6 Las Arenas Negras
An area above Garachico, popular with walkers who are keen to explore the island's youngest volcano (page 47)

7 Loro Parque
Zoo and shows in Puerto de la Cruz (page 41)

8 Masca
A remote village deep in the Teno gorge (page 48)

9 Punta de Teno
A lonely coastal region with a light house (page 48)

beside the church of the same name, houses a varied collection of Latin American art and arts and crafts. The museum pieces date from several centuries. The cellars house a collection of Canarian costumes. *Plaza Santo Domingo; Mon–Fri 9.30 am–6 pm; Sat 9.30 am–1 pm; Admission: 250 ptas*

RESTAURANTS

Engazo
This restaurant occupies an old house decorated in rustic style. Rabbit is a speciality. *Daily (except Tues) 1 pm–4 pm and 7 pm–12 midnight; situated in the La Luz district, behind the pottery museum; Category 3*

Las Caseosas
Canarian specialities in an old mansion with a pretty patio. *Daily 10 am–12 midnight; La Carrera, 21, below the Casas de los Balcones; Category 2*

SHOPPING

La Orotava is one of the best places to buy the 'open threadwork' embroidery called *calados*; nice hand-woven baskets in all shapes and sizes, as well as woodcarvings, can also be bought here.

Artesanía Balcón Canario
A well-stocked souvenir shop with plenty of hand made goods. *C/. Viera, 23, 25*

Casa de los Balcones
Table cloths, napkins, blouses and many other items, all with hand-embroidered decorations. *C/. San Francisco, 4*

Convento Molino
Offers a similar selection of souvenirs to the Casa de los Balcones, but also includes a picture gallery. *C/. San Francisco, 5*

Centro Comercial
This multi-storeyed shopping complex is at the bus station. Rows of small shops sell everyday items. *Avda. Benítez de Lugo*

HOTEL

Victoria
Since the opening of this hotel in a large, modernized manor house, La Orotava can boast of having comfortable accommodation. *12 rooms; C/. Hermano Apolinar 8; Tel: 33 16 83; Fax: 32 05 19; Category 3*

INFORMATION

Tourist information centre CIT
Daily 10 am–1 pm and 4 pm–7 pm; C/. Carrera, 1; Tel: 33 00 50; Fax: 33 39 11

PUERTO DE LA CRUZ

☛ City Map inside back cover

(**106/B-C1-2**) Situated at the far end of the Orotava valley, this fishing port has rapidly become the biggest tourist resort on the island. The numerous leisure activities make it an ideal holiday destination. However, the skies are often cloudy, especially in the winter. Puerto de la Cruz lies a good hour's drive from the southern airport. The town centre (pop. 27,000) is located beyond the botanical gardens and the peaceful, elegant La Paz district, where tourists stroll amongst the terraced cafés. A

THE NORTH-WEST COAST

50-m (164-foot)-high cliff separates this town quarter from the old central area beneath. Down below, the Atlantic waves wash upon the beach towards the grey hotel blocks so hurriedly erected in the 1960s when the tourist boom got underway. A promenade runs from La Paz, beside the sea, past the seawater swimming pools, across Calle de San Telmo and into the well-preserved town centre. Puerto de la Cruz had its origin as a harbour for La Orotava, to facilitate shipment of the valley's produce. In the early days, English and Portuguese traders settled here. Their prosperity led to the construction of some splendid houses and the town soon began to develop its own cultural scene. Nowadays, these grand old houses have been turned into hotels, restaurants and shops.

The heart of the old city is the recently renovated Plaza del Charco, shaded by its old, large trees. Locals and tourists congregate around the comfortable, terraced cafés, tended by scurrying waiters who never seem to stop for breath. Shoeshine boys and lottery ticket and newspaper salesmen mill amongst the clientele. During carnival and fiesta time, this is the hub of all the fun and celebrations. The nearby harbour also hums with activity, especially in the early morning when the fishermen disembark to unload their catch, which goes straight from the boat to the fish-stalls. During the winter months, high Atlantic waves surge toward the black lava coastline, making it too dangerous to swim in the surf. But swimmers can always enjoy the sea-water pool no matter what the weather is like. Playa Jardín, in the Punta Brava district, is a new beach with fine black sand and some attractive lawns, bars, restaurants and facilities. Centrally located is the revamped sandy beach of Playa Martiánez.

SIGHTS & MUSEUMS

Old Customs House
This traditional Canarian house was built back in 1620 by the founder of the harbour, Don Juan de Franchi. When Garachico harbour was destroyed, the customs officials of the Royal Treasury moved here. The house is now owned by the administrative office of the islands. A museum is in the planning. *C/. Lonjas*

Archaeological Museum
This interesting collection gives a moving account of the island's history. *In the old town's pedestrian zone. C/. del Lomo, 9A; Tues-Sat 9 am–1 pm and 5 pm–9 pm; Sun 9 am–1 pm*

Bananera El Guanche
Model banana plantation with souvenir shop. *On the main road towards the motorway; free bus every 20 minutes; daily 9.30 am–5.45 pm; Admission: 850 ptas*

Botanical Gardens
The idea of creating a botanical garden started during the reign of Carlos III. Experiments were carried out on cotton and tobacco plants, both of which thrived in the mild climate. Tropical plants from all over the

world were brought here in order to acclimatize them to a more European climate. The garden's main patron was the Marqués de Villanueva del Prado, who had a hill cleared near El Durazno and began planting in 1795. The climate turned out to be ideal and some examples of the plants that were cultivated then still exist. *Ctra. del Botánico, La Paz; daily 9 am–6 pm; Admission: 100 ptas*

Casa Iriarte

The birthplace of Tomás de Iriarte houses a maritime museum. The large rooms on the first floor of this mansion house models of ships from all over the world. On the ground floor Canarian embroidery is sold. *Corner of C/. San Juan and C/. Iriarte; daily except Sun and public holidays 9 am–7 pm; Admission: 200 ptas*

Castillo de San Felipe

This seaside fortress at the western end of the town was built in the early 1600s. It is now used for cultural events. *Paseo Luis Lavaggi*

Fishing port

Around 1800, there were a number of ports in Puerto de la Cruz, two for merchant shipping and several for smaller fishing boats. The biggest harbour, Puerto Viejo, lay to the west of the Castillo de San Felipe. At that time, the Barranco San Felipe widened out into a bay where boats could moor, however, this natural port was destroyed by a storm in 1826. All that remains are the two jetties of La Caleta harbour used only by a few fishing boats. The 500-m (1,640-foot)-long breakwater that stretches eastwards protects the harbour from the Atlantic waves. From here you can have a splendid ✹ view of the old town and of the mountains behind it.

Hotel Marquesa

This building was once the property of the Irish Cologan family, who ran a trading centre here. Amongst the illustrious guests who stayed here were Captain Cook and Alexander von Humboldt. It was eventually converted into a hotel in 1820. *C/. Quintana, 11*

San Amaro chapel

✹ The aristocratic Candia family from La Orotava worshipped San Amaro as their patron saint and benefactor, so in 1596 they built a small chapel in his honour on the cliff above Puerto de la Cruz. Years later, the Irishman Walsh-Valois acquired the site and named it La Paz to symbolize his strong yearning for peace. A platform opposite the chapel provides a fine view of the town below. On the right, a flight of steps leads up to a promenade with a café. *At the end of the Camino San Amaro*

San Telmo chapel

This chapel was founded by mariners in 1780 to honour their patron saint San Pedro González Telmo. The square around the chapel was once occupied by a fortress of the same name. The surviving wash-houses and wooden palisades were once part of the fortifications. *C/. San Telmo*

THE NORTH-WEST COAST

Pottery museum
Pieces of pottery have been gathered from all over Spain and are displayed here in this 16th-century feudal manor house. Adjacent to the collections is a pottery studio and a shop. *La Candia district, daily 10 am–4.45 pm, hourly bus service; Admission: 350 ptas*

Church of Nuestra Señora de la Peña de Francia
The present church was erected between 1684 and 1697, but the Baroque tower wasn't added until 1898. Of artistic interest are the pulpit, which was painted by de la Cruz y Ríos, and the altar figures by Estévez and Luján Pérez. The square outside is lined with palm trees and flowerbeds, and features a swan-like fountain.

PLEASURE PARKS

Free buses to the pleasure parks leave from opposite the former Café Columbus in the Avenida Colón.

Lago de Martiánez
A large sea-water swimming pool with islands and waterways. *Avda. Colón; Admission: 335 ptas, children: 170 ptas*

Loro Parque
★ Loro Parque is the island's main tourist attraction and boasts the biggest collection of parrots in the world. Visitors are also entertained with dolphin, sea lion and parrot shows. Recent additions include an 18-m (59-foot) shark tunnel, a Thai village, a bat cave and a gorilla enclosure. At lunchtime,

Dolphins in the Loro Parque

visitors can choose between a number of picnic areas, a café-restaurant and self-service restaurants. The bus service has been replaced by a miniature railway, which you board opposite the former Café Columbus. *In the Punta Brava district, daily 8.30 am–5 pm; Admission: 2,500 ptas, children: 1,250 ptas and discounts for groups*

Risco Bello
The moment you set foot on this park you will be overcome by a feeling of total relaxation and idleness. Sit down and enjoy the spacious lawns and gardens full of Canarian trees, shrubs and flowers. A café in the middle of the park is the ideal spot for a refreshing drink. *Next to the Casino Taoro, daily 11 am–9 pm*

Taoropark
The town's greenery extends up the hill in stages. This flower-filled park is another haven. It's hard to resist lingering on the park benches or under the shade of the old trees. Footpaths run

alongside a waterfall, and there is a ❖ viewing platform with a marvellous panorama of the town and the coastline.

RESTAURANTS

La Bodeguita
Down-to-earth restaurant serves wine from the barrel, ham and tapas. *Open all day; Plaza de Europa, opposite the town hall; Category 3*

La Boheme
A very elegant, high-quality restaurant. Speciality dishes. *Daily, near the Plaza del Charco, C/. Blanco, 5, 1st floor; Tel: 37 05 64; Category 1*

Mi vaca y yo
A typical Canarian restaurant that serves the island's specialities. *Daily (except Mon) 12 noon–3 pm and 7 pm–12 midnight; C/. Cruz Verde, 3; Category 2*

Régulo
This well-run establishment is located in a traditional Canarian house in the old town. Its rooms are small, comfortable and well decorated. In addition to the usual Canarian fare, you can sample mainland Spanish dishes. *C/. San Felipe; daily 12 noon–3 pm and 6 pm–11 pm; Category 2*

Taoro
❖ This restaurant offers one of the best views of all Puerto de la Cruz. The traditional Canarian cuisine, such as fresh fish and rabbit, is served here daily. *Open all day, in the Taoropark; directly below the Casino Taoro; Category 2*

SHOPPING

Arte Ponsjoan
Oil paintings of local landscape and island themes, for purchase directly from the artist. *C/. Quintana*

Galerie Colombe
Prints, lithographs, etchings, oils and exhibitions. *In the Canary Shopping Centre, La Paz district*

Karinia's silk painting
Delicate hand-painted scarves, blouses and other fashion items from real silk. *Sat and Sun 10 am–1 pm; La Paz district, C/. Aceviño, 45*

Handicrafts kiosk
Genuine Canarian handicrafts right next to the harbour mole.

Martiánez Center
This modern shopping centre is spread over two storeys and makes for an inviting place to shop or stroll through. Many elegant stores and boutiques sell a wide selection of goods. The complex also includes a large supermarket, bars, cafés and a small fun fair for children. Underground car park. *Daily 10 am–9 pm; below the San Felipe Hotel*

Mercado San Felipe
A modern, covered market-hall selling fruit, vegetables, meat and fish. The various shops are spread over three storeys. *Daily 9 am–1 pm and 4 pm–7 pm; Avda. Blas Pérez Gonzales, at the western end of the town*

Columbus Shopping Centre
A Canarian-style complex close to the Plaza del Charco. Several

THE NORTH-WEST COAST

restaurants and a string of attractive shops. *Daily 9 am–8 pm*

Visanta
Bazaar selling electronic novelties. *Avda. General Franco*

HOTELS

Many of the hotels in Puerto de la Cruz were built in the 1960s, when the tourist boom was getting underway and most of them are close to the town centre. Soon there was no space left to build there, so developers turned to neighbouring areas, such as the La Paz district. The advantage of the newer hotels is that they are in quiet, more attractive locations; the disadvantage is that they are far from the beach and the town centre. All hotels have swimming pools and a shuttle-bus service into town.

Botánico
Five-star luxury hotel with a superb garden and suites with private pools. Every imaginable amenity to match its rating. *282 rooms; opposite the Botanical Garden; Tel: 38 14 00; Fax: 38 15 04; Category 1*

Don Manolito
This is a hotel on the edge of the town centre, about a five-minute walk from Punta Brava. It is a family-run establishment with a friendly, informal atmosphere. All 49 rooms are well furnished and with balconies. Facilities include a swimming pool, a sun terrace and a bar lounge with TV. *C/. Dr. Madan; Tel: 38 50 12; Fax: 37 08 7; Category 3*

Los Geranios
A clean guest house; double room 2,500 ptas. *C/. del Lomo, 14; Tel: 38 28 10; Category 3*

Hotel/Apartamentos Maritim
This hotel and apartment block lies behind the Punta Brava district in an extremely quiet location beside the sea. The rooms are spacious and comfortably furnished. There are two swimming pools and several sun terraces. Plenty of sports and leisure activities. In-house disco. Hotel-owned buses. *451 rooms; Burgado, Los Realejos; Tel: 34 20 12; Fax: 34 21 09; Category 1*

Prinsotel La Chiripa Garden
A holiday complex in a quiet part of town on the edge of the Taoropark. Hidden away in a vast (30,000 sq m/322,920 sq foot), well-tended palm garden. It has two swimming pools, several sun terraces, two pool bars and a café-restaurant, a lounge with satellite TV and a wide choice of sport and entertainment facilities, so there's no chance of boredom setting in. There is even a health and fitness centre. The atmosphere is relaxed and very friendly. Hotel-owned buses. *362 rooms; Urb. San Fernando; Tel: 38 20 50; Fax: 38 08 93; Category 1*

Tigaiga
First-class hotel under Swiss management in the Taoropark. Exclusive atmosphere. *77 rooms; Tel: 38 32 51; Fax: 38 40 55; Category 2*

SPORTS & LEISURE

Fishing
The best spots for fishing are off the breakwater, by the old

fishing port and at the end of the Playa Martiánez.

Swimming
Lago de Martiánez
This architecturally quite impressive sea-water swimming pool consists of several pools linked together by waterways. In addition, there are large sun terraces surrounded by vegetation. Plenty of restaurants and bars offer a change of scenery.
Playa Jardín
★ Puerto de la Cruz's new 'garden beach' in the Punta Brava district below Loro Parque. Extensive sandy beach with huge gardens, a terraced café, a restaurant and other amenities.
Playa Martiánez
This beach, not far from the town centre, has recently been renovated. A wave machine operating below the surface simulates sea currents.

Health and fitness
La Chiripa, spa, sauna and sport studio. *Urb. San Fernando; Casablanca-Gym, Urb. El Tope; Bahamas-Gym, Avda. General Franco*

Covered wagon rides
Cañadas-Trek: a covered, horse-drawn wagon ride through Tenerife's beautiful forests. *3750 ptas, including meals; Tel: 908/ 10 99 71*

Squash
Squash centre inside the Edificio Belitope. *La Paz*

Diving
The *Atlantic* diving school in the Hotel Maritim. *Tel and Fax: 36 28 01*

Tennis
Most hotels have good tennis courts, some floodlit. There's also the *Tennis Center Miramar (Urb. Valparaiso; Los Realejos)*

Walking
Walkers and hikers follow either the marked paths or use one of the guidebooks for walking tours available in good bookshops. For guided walks, contact Gregorio at the *Hotel Tigaiga; Tel: 38 32 51*, or the *Alpine School Innsbruck*, at the *Hotel Bonanza; Tel: 38 11 00* (ask for 'Martin')

ENTERTAINMENT

Abaco
In this old, elegant manor house, you can enjoy your drinks listening to classical music. Concerts on Sat. *Daily from 8 pm; El Durazno, above the Botanical Gardens*

Andromeda/
Isla de Lago nightclub
An exclusive night club in the Lago de Martiánez area. Features a stainless-steel dance floor beneath a dome that can be opened to expose the stars. International performances and folklore evenings are also staged here. *Daily 9.30 pm–3 am; Avda. Colón; Admission: 3,850 ptas, with evening meal 6,000 ptas*

Caballo Blanco
❖ A local four-man band plays good dancing tunes in this rustic-style restaurant. Two comfortable bars are located away from the dance floor. Reasonable prices. *Daily 9 pm–3 am; Promenade San Telmo, Hotel San Telmo foyer*

THE NORTH-WEST COAST

Café de Paris
Terraced café and bistro with an international atmosphere directly on the promenade. A place to see and be seen. *Daily from 10 am until late; Avda. Colón*

Casino Taoro
Roulette and black jack in the Taoropark. *Daily from 9 pm; Ctra. Taoro; Admission: 500 ptas, identification required*

Rincón del Puerto
Canarian patio with various restaurants; *tapas*, country wine, fish specialities. Live music from 8 pm. *Daily from 10 am; by the Plaza del Charco (in the old town)*

Bar Tejas Verde
Canarian musicians play atmospheric music and songs for singing along. An authentic venue where native conviviality can be experienced in close quarters. *Daily 9 pm–1 am; C/. Puerto Viejo, 28*

Discoteca Victoria
In the Hotel Tenerife Playa, opposite the sea-water pool. The smart atmosphere attracts a middle-aged clientele. *Daily until 4 am*

INFORMATION

Oficina de Turismo
Plaza de Europa, by the town hall; Tel: 38 60 00; Fax: 37 02 43

SURROUNDING AREA

Aguamansa (107/D3)
★ High up, on the right-hand side of the road, just before it disappears in the pine forest, is a trout farm that is open to the public. There is also a forest information service giving information about the wildlife and the local habitat. Footpaths lead to La Caldera, a small crater and popular picnic spot, where barbecue grills have been installed.

Buenavista del Norte (104/B2)
This attractive, isolated village of 5,000 inhabitants is nestled in the midst of banana plantations at the end of the Isla Baja, directly beneath the steeply rising Teno hills. Locals meet in the pavilion to chat or play games in the square in the shade of the bay trees. Streets are lined with traditional houses. Sadly, the 16th-century church Nuestra Señora de los Remedios was destroyed by fire in 1996; the church will soon be rebuilt.

Behind the square, there is a road that leads down to a pebble beach where fishing boats are moored. About 1-km (½ mile) further west is the ↘ *Mirador de Don Pompejo*. This viewing platform opens up behind a rock gateway. On a clear day it is possible to make out the neighbouring island of La Palma and see the north coast as far as Puerto de la Cruz. The village restaurant of *La Cancela* is recommended, serving local food and good table wine. *Daily 12 noon–10 pm; Ctra. El Rincón 1; Category 3.*

Garachico (105/D2)
↘ The small, traditional village of Garachico (pop. 5,900) is about 25 km (16 miles) away from Puerto de la Cruz. Set in a picturesque spot on a lava peninsula, it exudes the atmosphere of a tranquil resort. Just

offshore is the striking Roque de Garachico, the village symbol. Formed from lava scree, the coast is flat and features a pretty promenade that follows the shoreline. At the western end, between the rocks, is a seawater pool. A monument to a lifeguard drowned in the spring of 1987, when an ocean earthquake caused tidal waves in the area, stands near the Castillo de San Miguel. This 16th-century fortress bears the coat-of-arms of the counts of Gomera and Adeje on its sturdy portal, and is one of the few buildings to have survived the eruption of 1706.

Founded after the Spanish conquest, Garachico evolved rapidly into a thriving commercial centre, helped by its harbour serving as an outlet for Tenerife's wine. This prosperity was brought to a sudden end when the Bermeka volcano erupted, spewing lava for 40 days and burying the opulent mansions of this flourishing port. A large part of the town and its harbour was completely destroyed; only the tower of the Santa Ana church survived unscathed. Inside the 18th-century church that now stands in its place, the Baroque altar and statues of St Anna and St Joachim by Luján Pérez are worth a closer look. On the *plaza* facing the church, stands a monument to Simón Bolívar, the 'liberator of South America'.

Directly behind the square lies the 17th-century palace of the counts of Gomera and Adeje, descendants of Cristóbal de Ponte, who founded the harbour around 1500. Another building that escaped the volcano's wrath is the former Franciscan monastery (Convento de San Francisco), now the Casa de Cultura. It is used for cultural events, when visitors can admire the fine interior and splendid cloisters. Recommended are the mini hotel *San Roque* in an old manor house *(12 rooms, C/. Esteban de Ponte, 33; Tel: 13 34 35, Category 3)* and the restaurant *Isla Baja*, known for its fresh fish and shellfish *(C/. Esteban de Ponte, 5; Category 3)*. Information available from the town hall *(daily 9 am–1 pm; Plaza de la Libertad, 1; Tel: 83 00 00; Fax: 83 13 01)*.

La Guancha (105/F2)

To reach La Guancha (pop. 5,000), take the beautiful road that leads from Realejo Alto up the steep Tigaiga incline to the rural village of Icod El Alto. Continue through the scented pine forests until you reach La Guancha, at the foot of the 896-m (2,940-foot)-high Topete. This town was renowned for its pottery and the skills of its craftsmen. Their know-how is being passed on at the handicrafts school that has been set up here.

The main thoroughfare is lined with neat, modern houses decorated with flowers. Agriculture remains the main source of income for La Guancha's inhabitants. The community recently opened a *casino*, where the local youth meet every Sunday afternoon for dancing. Exhibitions of local crafts are held here in the summer. A number of water galleries run along the slopes above the village.

THE NORTH-WEST COAST

Icod de los Vinos   (105/D-E2-3)
About 25 km (15 miles) west of Puerto de la Cruz lies the town of Icod de los Vinos (pop. 18,000), which dates back to 1501. As the name suggests, wines are produced in the nearby vineyards, which have earned a good reputation. The old town grew around the tiny church; today the town centre is dominated by the modern residential blocks of the eastern side.

Icod is an important destination for tourists because of its ancient ★*dragon tree*. This impressive example is over 16 m (52½ feet) high and 6 m (20 feet) wide. With both preservation and tourism in mind, it was deceided to protect the tree and the road to Santiago del Teide was re-routed. The road now leads through a tunnel that was built underneath the old town. Right next to the dragon tree you can visit the *Mariposario del Drago,* a butterfly park with hundreds of colourful and exotic butterflies *(daily 10 am–7.30 pm; Admission: 500 ptas)*. A little further along, behind the tree, lies the verdant Parque de Lorenzo Cáceres with the 16th-century church of San Marcos. One of the treasures held within the five-naved church is a priceless silver cross from Mexico, reckoned to be one of the finest examples of silver filigreed works in the world. It is on view only in the mornings.

There are two pavilions nearby and various types of palm tree, jacaranda and laurel, all casting their shadows over this peaceful spot. A flight of steps leads from the park up to the Plaza de la Constitución, flanked by some typically ornate houses.

A road winds through banana plantations to the black, sandy beach of ❂ *Playa de San Marcos*. The sea here is ideal for swimming, as the surf is not too rough and the current hardly noticeable. Do not be in too much of a hurry to get to the beach, as a pretty, stuccoed chapel can easily be overlooked. This entire rocky landscape is dotted with caves, some extending as far back as 40 m (130 feet).

In the district of El Amparo, the deepest cave of the Canary Islands, the *Cueva del Viento*, is found. Its full length has been measured at 14,870 m (48,800 feet). Unfortunately, it is not yet open to the public due to safety reasons, but there are plans to erect a research centre here, which will enable for visitors to explore the first 250 m (820 feet).

Above La Montañeta is the picnic area of ★*Las Arenas Negras*. This is a popular spot with locals and tourists alike, so barbecue grills have been set up for public use. It is also a good starting point for walks to the island's youngest volcano, the Chinyero.

The following dining establishments in Icod are recommended: the *Cafetería Brisamar (corner of Avda. Marítima and C/. San Marcos; Category 3)* and the restaurant *Caney (Los Moriscos; Category 3)*. Information available at the town hall *(daily 9 am– 2 pm; Plaza Luis de León Huerta; Tel: 81 07 58; Fax: 81 06 69)*.

The black sand of Playa de San Marcos near Icod de los Vinos

Masca (104/B-C4)
★ The tiny village of Masca lies in a wide dip of the Teno hills, and consists of just a few houses and farmsteads. An asphalt road has been laid that now connects the village with the outside world and some tourist buses now include it in their itinerary. In the town centre, there is a small church and the palm-shaded central square. A small museum in Lomo de Masca records the history of this once remote settlement, until recently accessible only by bridle paths.

Mirador Garachico (105/D2-3)
This viewpoint on the road from Icod de los Vinos to Santiago del Teide affords a good view of Garachico.

Mirador Humboldt (106/C1)
This panorama, named after Alexander von Humboldt, lies on the country road between La Orotava and Santa Úrsula. It was here that the German explorer and naturalist declared his enthusiasm for the Orotava valley shadowed by the volcanic Teide, and a plaque in Spanish records his words. The view is unforgettable; sadly, as more and more tourists have made this their destination, the countryside is not as unspoilt as it was in Humboldt's day.

Punta de Teno (104/A3)
★ ◎ In order to reach this remote, flat coastal region and its lighthouse from Buenavista, it is necessary to pass through two road tunnels. Several tranquil bays lie hidden along the craggy coastline dotted with countless caves. When the waves roar in, the compressed air on the cavities pushes the water out with great force, recalling giant fountains. Fishing boats moor beside the light house and there is also a black sandy beach for swimmers.

Los Realejos (106/B2)
Los Realejos (pop. 30,000) is in reality comprised of two districts, Realejo Alto and Realejo Bajo, both lying on the steep slopes of the western Orotava valley. Realejo Alto (the 'upper

THE NORTH-WEST COAST

Realejo') boasts some well-preserved Canarian houses and the oldest church in Tenerife, Santiago Apóstol. It is believed that the first Guanches were baptized here. The Gothic belltower is covered by Oriental-style shingles. The church altarpiece was painted by an artist of the Flemish school. Directly behind the town hall, a narrow street leads to the cemetery, its entrance marked by a wonderful dragon tree.

Realejo Bajo (the 'lower Realejo') is a modern town with some new residential blocks and attractive cafés. El Socorro is the only proper beach here. Throughout the year, powerful waves crash on the shore, making it a popular haunt for surfers – only good swimmers and those who are familiar with the surf here should venture out into the strong currents. A number of fish restaurants with car parking facilities can also be found in the vicinity. Access to the beach is from the northern coastal road in the direction of Icod de los Vinos, and the exit has a sign.

The coastal region is occupied by a number of holiday developments, namely Romántica I, Romántica II, La Longuera (with shops) and El Toscal. In the district of La Montañeta, a hill of volcanic ashes is crowned by a tiny white chapel, a popular destination for the locals. On the road to La Luz stands a veritable jewel of Canarian architecture in the form of an old monastery with a magnificent inner courtyard. Now restored paying fastidious attention to detail and at considerable cost, the building has been converted into a popular restaurant known appropriately as ==El Monasterio.== Quite apart from the food, the vaulting in the cellars and the vast range of wines, the setting makes this a worthwhile visit. The menu is varied, featuring mainly meat dishes, and prices are very reasonable. *(open from 10 am; Category 2)*. Also recommended is the *Villa Nueva* restaurant for its elegant yet friendly atmosphere. International and Canarian dishes are served *(daily, except Wed; 12 noon– 3 pm and 6 pm–11 pm; San Vicente; Category 1)*. One hotel is worth mentioning: *Tierra de Oro*, a spa hotel located in a quiet spot at the edge of town, it offers 80 beds, a vegetarian restaurant and a medical consultant, who'll recommend a course of treatment upon request. *(Tel: 34 10 00; hotel buses; Category 2)*.

Los Silos (104/C2)

This pretty village (pop. 5,400) lies on the Isla Baja. By the plaza, a small 20th-century church built in the Neo classical style, Nuestra Señora de la Luz, houses a figure of the Cristo de la Misericordia (17th century), sculpted by Juan de Mesa of Seville. To reach the coast, which is only 2 km (1 mile) away, turn off by the petrol station at the far end of the village. There are a number of modern developments here as well as a sea-water pool. A narrow road winds amongst the banana plantations along the lava coast and leads to the minuscule fishing village of La Caleta, where you'll find a small black sand beach.

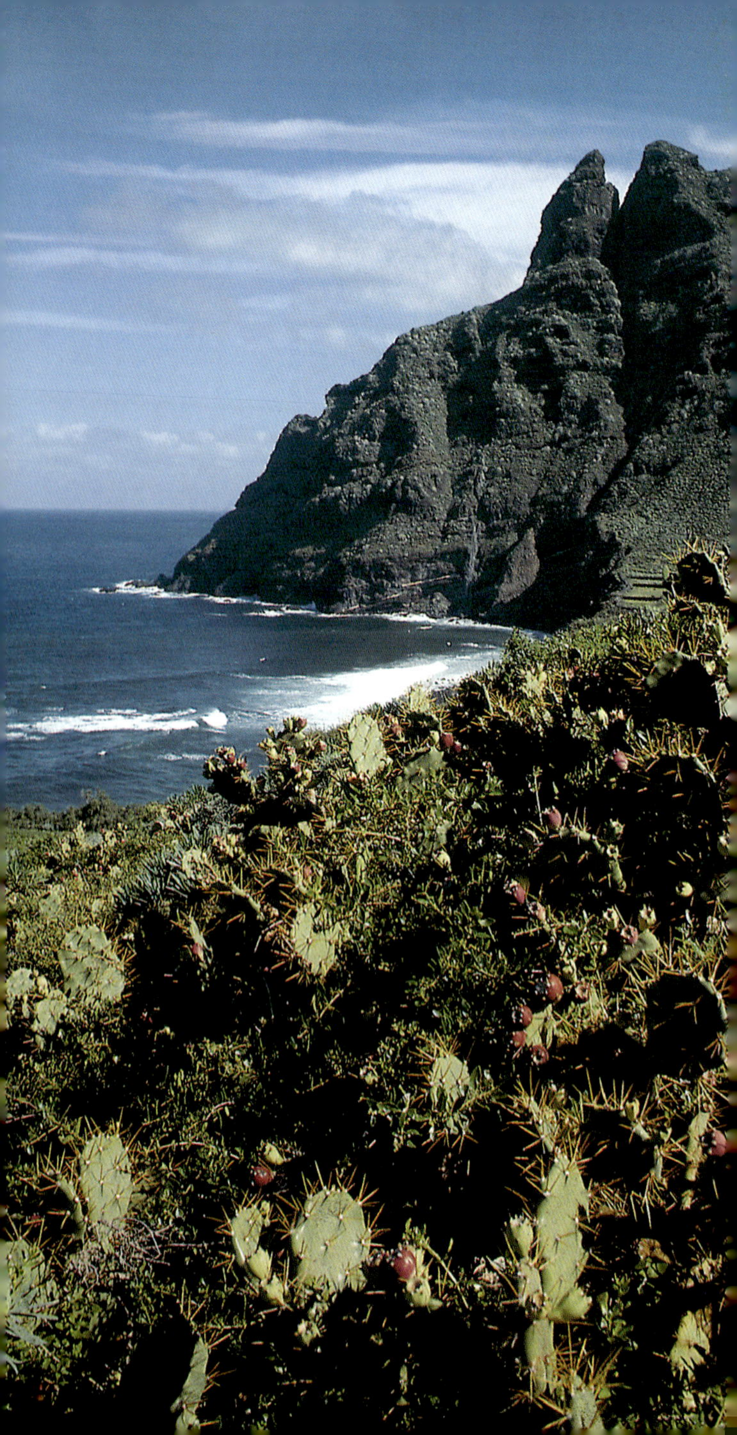

THE NORTH-EAST COAST

Cliffs and chasms

Hikers will be rewarded with some stunning views in this rugged part of the island

The stretch of coastline between Santa Úrsula and Tacoronte is bordered with cliffs, averaging around 200 m (650 feet) in height. The landscape, furrowed by deep gorges or *barrancos*, rises gently up towards the ridge that forms the mountain's backbone, an area known as the Cumbre Dorsal. The slopes are cultivated with terraced fields and scattered with villages and hamlets. The Cumbre Dorsal reaches its highest point at 2,000 m (6,564 feet), where the giant crater of Las Cañadas is, and drops down to 600 m (1,970 feet), where it levels out onto the plain of La Laguna. A band of clouds lingers often over the flat terrain, so La Laguna is overcast most of the time. To the north, the plain dips down to the sea via the Valle de Guerra and the Valle de Tejina, while to the south lies the 5-km (3-mile)-wide bay of Santa Cruz de Tenerife, where huge cargo vessels dock. The climate in this sheltered bay is hot and humid. The jagged peaks of the grey Anaga mountain range form a stunning backdrop to the Santa Cruz skyline. Rising in places to 1,000 m (3,300 feet), its lower slopes and inaccessible valleys covered by dense laurel forests, the Anagas dominate the far north-eastern corner of the island.

BAJAMAR

(**102/A2**) This quiet, popular resort lies between the foothills of the Anagas and the sea. Both sides of the valley are lined with houses, hotel complexes and bungalows. A promenade along the coast leads to a seawater pool. There is a small, black sandy beach nearby, but the strong surf makes it difficult to swim. For day hikers, the Anaga mountains are easily accessible from here. Their steep rock faces dominate the surrounding landscape.

HOTELS

Delfín
Convenient, centrally located hotel complex situated by the

Hedges of prickly-pear cacti cover the rugged cliffs of the north-east coast

MARCO POLO SELECTION: THE NORTH-EAST COAST

1 The Anaga massif
A popular destination for walkers and day-trippers. One of the island's most secluded and attractive landscapes (page 58)

2 Cumbre Dorsal
Stunning views from the panoramic road on top of the island's backbone (pages 58)

3 Nuestra Señora de la Concepción
A magnificent church in La Laguna with a Mudéjar tower and some exquisite works of art (page 53)

4 Flea market in Santa Cruz
A treasure trove for bargain hunters (page 57)

5 Casa del Vino
Wine museum set inside a 16th-century mansion in El Sauzal, with a tasting room and restaurant serving regional specialities (page 60)

6 Playa de las Teresitas
Located near San Andrés, this is the longest and most beautiful beach in Tenerife. The sand was imported from the Sahara (page 54)

sea, with video and discotheque bar, tennis courts and a freshwater swimming pool in the gardens. *66 rooms; Avda. del Sol, 39; Tel: 54 02 00; Fax: 54 02 00; Category 1*

Océano
Well-run hotel with a magnificent garden to relax in and enjoy the fresh air. There is also a health centre offering a variety of nutritional programmes. Be sure to try and book one of the 100 apartments that have an ocean view. *Punta del Hidalgo; Tel: 54 11 12; Category 2*

INFORMATION

Ayuntamiento
Daily 9 am–2 pm; La Plaza; Tel: 54 11 20

LA LAGUNA

(102/A-B3-4) La Laguna (pop. 110,000) lies on a broad, flat plain, an unusual geographical feature for the northern part of the island. The narrow streets are laid out in a chequer-board pattern, with many old houses and mansions. Some date back to 1497, when Alonso Fernández de Lugo founded La Laguna and made it the island's capital. A Neo classical town hall stands in the shady Plaza del Adelantado; the old chapels, churches, monasteries and cathedrals house many priceless art treasures. The only bishop in the Canary Islands has his residence here. The modern campus of the University of La Laguna, located mostly around the town centre, serves

THE NORTH-EAST COAST

SIGHTS

Cathedral
When La Laguna became a bishopric in 1818, renovation work started immediately to convert the Los Remedios parish church into a cathedral. Worth seeing are the pulpit, the side altars with statues by Luján Pérez and exquisite silverwork. Behind the high altar lies the grave of the town's founder, Alonso Fernández de Lugo. *C/. Obispo Rey Redondo*

Nuestra Señora de la Concepción
★ This church is indeed one of the Tenerife's artistic treasures. The tower of this 16th-century church was built wholly in the Mudéjar style. The wooden interior, although a little gloomy, has a splendid pulpit made of carved cedar and statues by Estévez. *C/. Obispo Rey Redondo*

Museo de la Ciencia y del Cosmos
Since it opened in 1993, this natural science museum has been taking a look at the universe in fascinating, and often disconcerting, displays explaining the solar system, the appearance of life on earth and the relationship between mankind and the cosmos. Visitors are invited to watch a series of exciting experiments. *Vía Láctea, s/n; daily (except Mon) 10 am–8 pm; Admission: 200 ptas*

RESTAURANTS

La Gotera
Restaurant serving typical Canarian dishes. *Daily 1 pm–4 pm and 8 pm–0.20 am; San Agustín; Category 2*

HOTEL

Nivaria
New house in the town centre. *60 rooms; Plaza del Adelantado, 11, Tel: 26 42 98; Fax: 25 96 34; Category 2*

INFORMATION

Ayuntamiento
C/. Obispo Rey Redondo, 1; Tel: 60 11 00; Fax: 60 11 02

LA MATANZA DE ACENTEJO

(**101/D-E4**) La Matanza means 'the slaughter', and refers to a battle that took place on 31 May 1494, when the Spanish suffered a humiliating defeat in their first confrontation with the Guanches. Two hills are the symbol for this village (pop. 5,000), which extends from the coast to a forest known as Bosque de la Esperanza. The surrounding region is renowned for its wine. Perched on rocks, the village of El Caletón is separated from the sea by a small, black sandy beach. Further up, on the edge of the cliff, the apartment blocks of El Puntillo del Sol, a holiday village, cling to the rocks. The main village lies above the motorway. The restaurants and bars along the old road offer some fine views over the north-west coast.

MUSEUMS

Museo Cooperativa AYT-M-Maheh
Here, in the old town hall, the history of traditional Canarian

sports, such as stick fighting, stone-lifting and the still popular *lucha canaria* (wrestling). *C/. Real; daily (except Mon) 9.30 am–1 pm and 3.30 pm–6 pm; Admission: 200 ptas, with performance 400 ptas*

RESTAURANTS

Casa Juan
Smoked salmon, eel and mackerel are speciality dishes of this attractively furnished, family-run restaurant. *Tues–Sat 12.30 pm–4 pm and 6.30 pm– 10.30 pm; Camino de Acentejo, 29; Category 2*

San Diego
A former horse stable was converted into a very comfortable restaurant. Tasty, pricey Canarian dishes. *Daily 1 pm–4 pm and 7 pm–12 midnight; C/. General del Norte; Category 3*

INFORMATION

Ayuntamiento
Ctra. General; Tel: 57 71 97; Fax: 57 78 71

PUNTA DEL HIDALGO

(**102/A–B1**) A peaceful holiday resort, at its heart, it's still a typical fishing village. To enable tourists to reach this rather inaccessible spot, the Anaga rocks had to be blasted to make way for the road. The hotels on the flat peninsula next to the rocky coastline have sea-water swimming pools and the reefs are ideal for sea-fishing. About 1 km (½ mile) beyond the village, the road ends with a round about. This vantage point offers a fine view out over the eastern edge of the Anaga mountains and the rocky offshore island of Dos Hermanos. Punta del Hidalgo is a good starting point for walking tours of the Anagas.

RESTAURANT/CAFÉ

La Caseta
Specialities include fresh fish and Canarian dishes. *Daily 11 am–11 pm; Avda. Marítima; Category 3*

Café Melita
☪ A well-run café with a magnificent panoramic view; a large selection of cakes and pastries. *Ctra. La Punta, daily from 10 am*

INFORMATION

Ayuntamiento
Daily 9 am–2 pm; La Plaza; Tel: 54 11 20

SAN ANDRÉS

(**103/D3**) With its squares and steep mountain slopes studded with pretty, white houses, this picturesque fishing village resembles an Indian pueblo and is certainly worth a visit. The ruins of a watchtower that was built to forewarn islanders of pirate attacks can be seen in the outskirts. A little further on, Saharan sand gleams in the sun. This yellow sand was transported here from Africa in the 1970s to fulfil the expectations of the growing number of tourists. It is known as the ★ *Playa de las Teresitas*. Shade is supplied by clusters of of palm trees, and an embankment protects bathers from the rough surf. The 2 km (1 mile) - long beach is

THE NORTH-EAST COAST

dominated to the west by the rocky slopes of the Anaga mountains. The coastal road to the north-east winds its way up to the impressive panorama at ❧ Punta de los Órganos. From this point, the eastern coastline all the way to Candelaria is visible. The black sand beaches of Playa de Burro and the nudist Playa Las Gaviotas lie to the east.

RESTAURANT

La Langostera
Fish and shellfish in a pleasant, relaxed atmosphere. *Daily (except Monday) 12 noon–11 pm; Avda. El Dique, 14*

INFORMATION

Oficina de Turismo
Cabildo, daily 9 am–1 pm and 4 pm–7 pm; Plaza de España; Tel: 60 55 00; Fax: 60 57 81

SANTA CRUZ DE TENERIFE

☛ City Map inside back cover

(**102/B-C4**) The more attractive side of this large port city (pop. 200,000) is not evident at first sight, but once you begin exploring you'll soon discover many historic squares and buildings, parks and boulevards, as well as futuristic multi-storeyed blocks housing many banks and offices. Santa Cruz, capital city, trading and distribution centre, is situated in a sheltered bay at the foot of the Anaga massif and owes its importance to the development of its port. It has been one of Spain's main ports since the mid-1600s. Santa Cruz has a long history: on 3 May 1492, the conquistadors landed on what was then Añaza beach, built their first fortress there and proceeded to conquer

Tons of yellow sand from the Sahara Desert were shipped over to embellish the Playa de las Teresitas near San Andrés

the rest of the island. With the destruction of Garachico, Santa Cruz took its place. Still, it was exposed to pirate attacks, so new fortifications were added and a military governor appointed. On 25 July 1797, one year after the port was granted exclusive trading rights with the New World, Admiral Nelson attacked. His objective: to capture two galleons laden with Mexican silver. During the ensuing battle, Nelson lost his right arm. In 1822, Santa Cruz became the capital of all the Canary Islands.

SIGHTS

Harbour
Ships from all over Europe, the Americas, Africa and Asia dock here. Tankers unload their cargoes at the refinery to the west of the city. Several jetfoils and ferries leave for Gran Canaria every day.

Nuestra Señora dela Concepción
With a foundation stone laid as far back as 1502 by the Spanish conquistadors, this church is the oldest in Santa Cruz, but in 1652 it fell victim to fire and was not fully restored until the 18th century. The interior of the five-naved church was completed in ornate Baroque style. Important are the 'Dolorosa' figures by Luján Pérez, the 'Concepción' by Estévez at the high altar and the carved choir stalls. The cross that the conquistadors planted on the beach and a Gothic statue of the Virgin Mary are kept here, together with the flags that Admiral Nelson left behind. After recent restoration, the church has opened its doors once again. *C/. Domínguez Alfonso, by the Barranco de Santos*

Parque Municipal García Sanabria
Named after the popular mayor who designed this park between 1925 and 1930, the park has statues of the island's famous artists and citizens amid native trees and bushes. *C/. Méndez Núñez*

Plaza de la Candelaria
This lovely rectangular square bordered by benches and shops is a pedestrian zone. The statue in the centre of the square was sculpted by Antonio Canova in 1778 using Carrara marble. It depicts the Canarian patron saint looking down on four Guanche chieftains.

Plaza de España
The cruciform monument commemorating the dead of the Spanish Civil War (Monumento de los Caídos) can be seen here; a fine view of the city and harbour awaits visitors who take the lift to the top.

Plaza de Weyler
A beautiful marble fountain forms the centrepiece of this square. Star-shaped paths interspersed with flowerbeds all converge towards it. In the background stands the Neo classical building of the Capitanía General, erected by Gen. Valeriano Weyler at the end of the 19th century.

MUSEUMS

Museo Arqueológico
Items excavated from Guanche caves (tools, cutlery, weapons

THE NORTH-EAST COAST

and mummies) can be seen here. *C/. Fuente Morales, Mon–Sat 10 am–6 pm; Sun 10 am–2 pm; Admission: 200 ptas*

Museo Municipal de Bellas Artes
An extensive art gallery featuring paintings by Brueghel, Jordaens and Ribera (amongst others), as well as sculptures, weapons and coins from previous centuries, can be seen here. The library is on the upper floor. *C/. José Murphy, 4; daily 1 pm–7 pm; Admission: free*

RESTAURANTS/CAFÉ

El Áiguila
A favourite meeting place with a nice terrace. It offers many small dishes, but especially *paella*; and for dessert, cakes and ice-cream. *Daily 10 am–12 midnight; at the end of the C/. San José, Category 2*

Café del Príncipe
A wide selection of cakes; snacks are served in the garden café. *Daily 9 am–12 midnight; Plaza del Príncipe; Category 2*

Viva México
The name says it all: this is the place for Mexican specialities. *Tues–Sun 1 pm–4.30 pm and 8 pm–1 am; Parque La Granja, Avda. Madrid; Category 2*

SHOPPING

Calle del Castillo
This pedestrian zone is Tenerife's best shopping street.

Flea market
★ ❂ The flea market is held every Sunday morning around the Mercado de Nuestra Señora de África from 9 am to 2 pm. Everything from cheap junk to quality goods is sold.

Mercado de Nuestra Señora de África
❂ This Oriental-style building houses the fresh fruit, vegetable, meat and fish market. This is the place to experience authentic Tenerife. In a nearby lane lined with covered stalls, traders sell everything from cheap souvenirs to chamber pots. Expect to haggle. *C/. San Sebastián*

HOTELS

Santa Cruz is no tourist resort, so the hotels listed here are primarily for business people.

Atlántico
A new hotel situated right in the city centre, but in the pedestrian zone away from all the traffic noise. *60 rooms; C/. del Castillo; Tel: 24 63 75; Fax: 24 63 78; Category 2*

Mencey
This is indeed the top hotel of the city. Stylishly furnished with a swimming pool and set in a delightful garden. This is where King Juan Carlos and Queen Sofía often stay during their visits to Tenerife. *286 rooms; C/. Dr. José Neveiras, 38; Tel: 27 67 00; Fax: 28 00 17; Category 1*

ENTERTAINMENT

A Bordo
Café-Restaurant with plenty of atmosphere. *Avda. Anaga*

Discoteca KU
The best, most cosmopolitan disco in Santa Cruz. *Parque La Granja*

Olé
Bar/pub. *Rambla General Franco*

Vips
Bar/pub. *Rambla General Franco*

INFORMATION

Oficina de Turismo
Daily 9 am–1 pm and 4 pm–7 pm; Cabildo, Plaza de España; Tel: 60 55 00; Fax: 60 57 81

SURROUNDING AREA

The Anaga massif (102–103/A–E2)
★ ↘ The Anaga massif covers practically all of north-eastern Tenerife. This craggy and jagged mountain range is furrowed with deep valleys and gorges. On all three sides, the mountains drop precipitously down to the sea. The highest peak, the *Taborno*, is 1,024 m (3,361 feet) high. Although wild and deserted, it is one of the most beautiful parts of the island. The lower slopes, densely overgrown with laurels, form the Bosque de las Mercedes. Tree heath and broom take over at 800 m (2,600 feet), while moss and lichen coat the bare basalt rocks that tower up to the sky.

There's a picturesque drive north that's worth taking. It leaves from La Laguna and passes though the mountain village of Las Mercedes. The first viewpoint you reach is the *Mirador de Jardina* in a road bend above Las Mercedes. A few kilometres down the road is the guest house and pilgrims' chapel of *Cruz del Carmen*, located in a forest clearing. After about another kilometre, the road branches off to the right, in the direction of the *Pico del Inglés*. From the top of this peak you can see a panorama of the massif all the way to the Teide, and if it's exceptionally clear you can even see neighbouring Gran Canaria. The road continues uphill along the ridge, offering view after view of the coastline. At the junction, carry straight on to the restaurant of *El Bailadero* and on to the 'island's tip', to Chamorga. To reach the actual tip, continue on foot until you reach the abandoned lighthouse and a small sandy beach. At the junction mentioned above, instead of driving to Chamorga, you can turn left and follow the road that takes you through a tunnel. Soon you'll see Taganana on the northern coast, dotted with white houses. Stop for a glass of the excellent wine in one of the many *bodegas*. A few kilometres beyond Taganana's cobbled streets is the *Los Roques* beach, where the fish restaurants that cling to the rocks do a good trade with the tourists. The village of Almáciga sits on a small sandy beach about a kilometre further on. Return through the tunnel and head south across the peninsula through wild terrain and downhill to San Andrés on the opposite coast.

Cumbre Dorsal (106–107/B-F1-4)
★ ↘ The good, panoramic road that follows the narrow Cumbre Dorsal mountain range divides

THE NORTH-EAST COAST

the island into two. It offers some fine views as it rises from 600 to 2,300 m (2,000 to 7,500 feet) above sea level, where the giant Cañadas crater begins. Get off the motorway near La Laguna and follow the signs to La Esperanza. The sides of the road are lined with yellow and white broom until you reach La Esperanza, a village where sheep and pigs are bred. From this point on, the road is shaded by eucalyptus trees and Canarian pines that release a refreshing scent. About 4 km (2 ½ miles) further, a small restaurant and picnic site called *Las Raíces* comes into view. Take a break near *Montaña Grande* to enjoy a bird's-eyes view of Santa Cruz de Tenerife, La Laguna and the northern airport way below. Further on, *Mirador Ortuño* provides a marvellous opportunity to survey the northern half of the island. Turn right towards *Mirador de las Cumbres* a short distance on and, after about 200 m (650 feet), the southern half of the island becomes visible. On a clear day, Gran Canaria may appear out of the clouds. After a further 700 m (2,300 feet), the north coast emerges, at which point you may be able to pick out the western island of La Palma through the haze. The vegetation becomes sparser, and dense pine forests flank both sides of the road, which meanders through a gorge and gives you a chance to study the colourful volcanic rock formations. The white buildings of the Izaña meteorological observatory point skyward like a row of rockets. El Portillo and the Cañadas crater lie just ahead.

Radazul (102/B5)

This little town straddles the motorway and has developed into a popular resort for tourists and affluent young locals in recent years. The residential blocks, apartments and expensive villas are owned mainly by wealthy islanders. Luxury yachts are moored in the marina *Club de Mar Radazul*, which is sheltered by a 100-m (330-foot)-cliff and can accommodate about 100 boats. Most of the mooring places are occupied by local boats for long-term storage and consequently very few outsiders can stop over. Entering the port is easy, even at night, for the breakwater stands out clearly against the cliffs and the tall apartment blocks.

Tabaiba (102/A5)

About 8 km (5 miles) south of Santa Cruz, the motorway passes throughTabaiba. There are small businesses on the water's edge, while to the north a number of locally owned holiday villas have been built.

SANTA ÚRSULA

(101/D5) This rather modest village of 8,500 inhabitants has a church with some fine ceiling paintings and a lovely little palm-shaded square. Handicraft workshops and bars line the main thoroughfare and an old wine-press stands by the La Quinta motorway exit. In order to reach the viewpoint of *Vista Paraíso* on the rocks 260 m (853 feet) above the town, take the La Orotava motorway exit. The bridge over the motorway leads to the villa quarter.

RESTAURANTS

Los Corales
↙ Good fish and seafood, plus a panoramic view. *Daily 1 pm–4 pm and 7 pm–12 midnight; Cuesta de la Villa, 60; Category 2*

Vista Paraíso
↙ Café with panoramic terrace, perilously positioned at the top of the cliff. Renowned for its homemade cakes and tarts; good for savoury snacks, too. *Daily (except Sunday) 10 am–7 pm*

INFORMATION

Ayuntamiento
Plaza General Franco, 13; Tel: 30 00 25; Fax: 30 16 40

EL SAUZAL

(**101/E4**) The prettiest route to this village (pop. 6,200) located on the edge of the 300-m (985-foot)-high crag is via the Valle de los Ángeles. Leave the motorway at La Matanza de Acentejo and turn downhill to the right, past El Puntillo del Sol and Los Naranjeros. The steep, narrow coastal road down to the harbour of El Sauzal, Puertito de Sauzal, is fairly adventurous and literally breathtaking at stages, therefore not for the faint-hearted. The village is noted for its Moorish-style domed church. Near the monastery turn-off, a 16th-century mansion built beneath a huge boulder houses the wine museum ★ *Casa del Vino (daily 11 am–8 pm; Admission: free)*. There's a tasting room, a restaurant and a terraced café with a breathtaking ↙ view of the north coast.

SIGHT

Las Tosquillas
Botanical gardens with innumerable carnations, 50 different species of palm tree from all over the world and many exotic, colourful birds. *Daily 9 am–5 pm; C/. San Nicolás, 105; Admission: 700 ptas*

RESTAURANT

San Nicolás
Fish restaurant offering a very wide selection of fresh catch. *Daily (except Tues) 12 noon–12 midnight; Ctra. General de Sauzal; Category 3*

INFORMATION

Ayuntamiento
C/. de la Constitución, 3; Tel: 57 00 00; Fax: 57 09 73

TACORONTE

(**101/E3-4**) This busy market town of 17,000 inhabitants is situated in one of the island's most fertile regions. The wine, potatoes and other vegetables produced here are sold in the market at very reasonable prices. After passing the market, the same road takes you directly to the town centre, where the 17th-century church of San Agustín houses one of the island's most venerated statues of Christ (Cristo de los Dolores). Diagonally opposite the church stands a fine specimen of dragon tree. Hidden away in the lower part of town is

THE NORTH-EAST COAST

the church of Santa Catalina with its Mudéjar-style tower (17th-18th century). The interior has a beautifully carved ceiling panel, the 'Inmaculada' by Luján Pérez, a picture of the 'Ánimas' from Quintana and a high altar richly ornamented with intricate Mexican silverwork. Outside, the square is lined with Indian laurel trees. About 2 km (1 mile) down the road towards Valle de Guerra, turn left down the winding road that leads you straight to the beaches of Mesa del Mar and El Prix.

RESTAURANT

El Campo
Both the dishes and the atmosphere in this establishment are truly Canarian. *Daily 1 pm–12 midnight; Ctra. General, 350; Los Naranjeros; Category 3*

INFORMATION

Policía Municipal
Plaza del Cristo; Tel: 56 13 50; Fax: 56 25 90

VALLE DE GUERRA

(**101/F2-3**) The fertile valley and the village itself were named after a war hero, whose loyal services and accomplishments were rewarded by being given this valuable land after the conquest of Alonso Fernández de Lugo. Bananas and strelitzia grow abundantly here. Just outside the village, you will come to the early 18th-century residence that once belonged to the aristocratic Guerra family. The large house has now been successfully transformed into a local history museum, *Museo Casa de la Carta*.

MUSEUM

Museo Etnográfico
This is a historically interesting museum that shows how the islanders lived during the colonial era. *Daily (except Friday) 10 am–1 pm and 4 pm–6 pm; Admission: 200 ptas*

INFORMATION

Ayuntamiento
La Laguna, C/. Obispo Rey Redondo, 1; Tel: 26 10 11

LA VICTORIA DE ACENTEJO

(**101/D5**) This unassuming little village of 7,100 inhabitants is home to craftsmen, farmers and wine-growers. It is best known for its church, whose interior has a beautiful ornate silver altar from Mexico and an extensively carved wooden ceiling in the Mudéjar style.

RESTAURANT

Los Garrafones
Here you can savour typical Canarian dishes prepared according to old recipes. *Daily 12 noon–4 pm and 7 pm–10 pm; C/. Laureles, 2; Category 3*

INFORMATION

Ayuntamiento
Plaza Rodríguez Lara; Tel: 58 00 31; Fax: 58 01 76

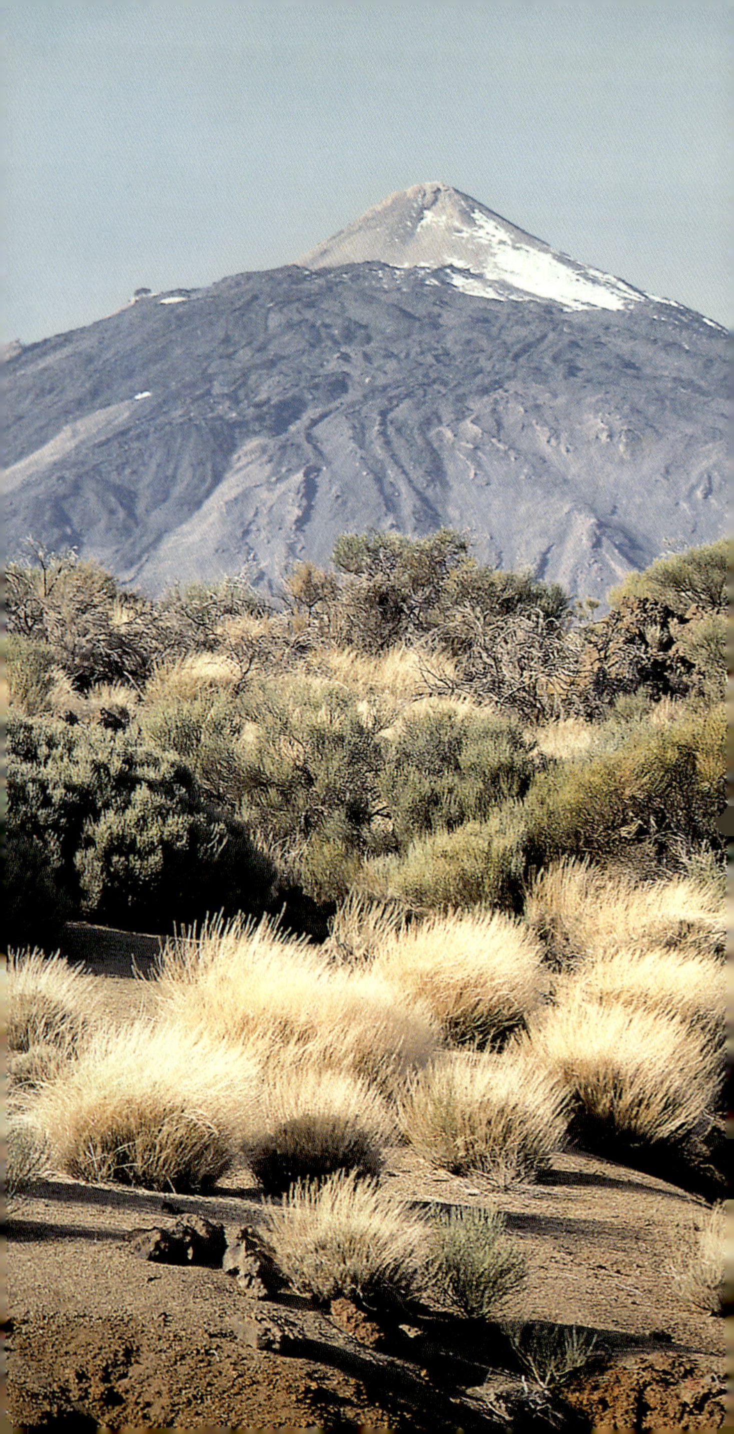

NATIONAL PARK

A lunar landscape

This spectacular volcanic backdrop took shape more than a quarter of a million years ago

The road from Puerto de la Cruz passes through La Orotava, and shortly thereafter comes to Aguamansa. The road crosses a dense pine forest, until 46 km (28½ miles) later you reach El Portillo, located in the ★ *Parque Nacional de las Cañadas del Teide* (**105/E-F4-6, 106/A-C4-6**) in the heart of Tenerife. This is also where the visitor centre (*centro de visitantes*) is located, which presents interesting information about the geological, biological and historical characteristics of this national park. The information is supplemented by a multilingual slide and sound presentation. As soon as you've left behind the plateau covered by pumice stone at the park's entrance, you see the stony desert of the Caldera de las Cañadas below a deep blue sky. This volcanic depression was formed by the collapse of the volcano's cone, and is known in geology as a caldera. This depression, also known as the original crater, lies at an altitude of 2,000 m (6,500 feet). On the northern side of the crater stands the 3,718-m (12,202-foot)-high Pico del Teide; to the south the crater is flanked by steep cliffs that rise to a height of 500 m (1,640 feet). With a circumference of 17 km (10½ miles), this vast nature reserve covers a total surface area of 13,571 hectares (33,534 acres), it was created in 1954 and is Spain's largest.

Scientists believe that the caldera was probably formed more than 300,000 years ago. Where the caldera now stands, a 3,000-m (9,850-foot)-high mountain was in its place. According to one theory, this mountain was a shield volcano having a relatively thin outer rock layer, which any moment would give way to pressure from the liquid rock bubbling beneath it. Therefore, the

The Pico del Teide, the 'Roof of Tenerife', dominates the island's landscape

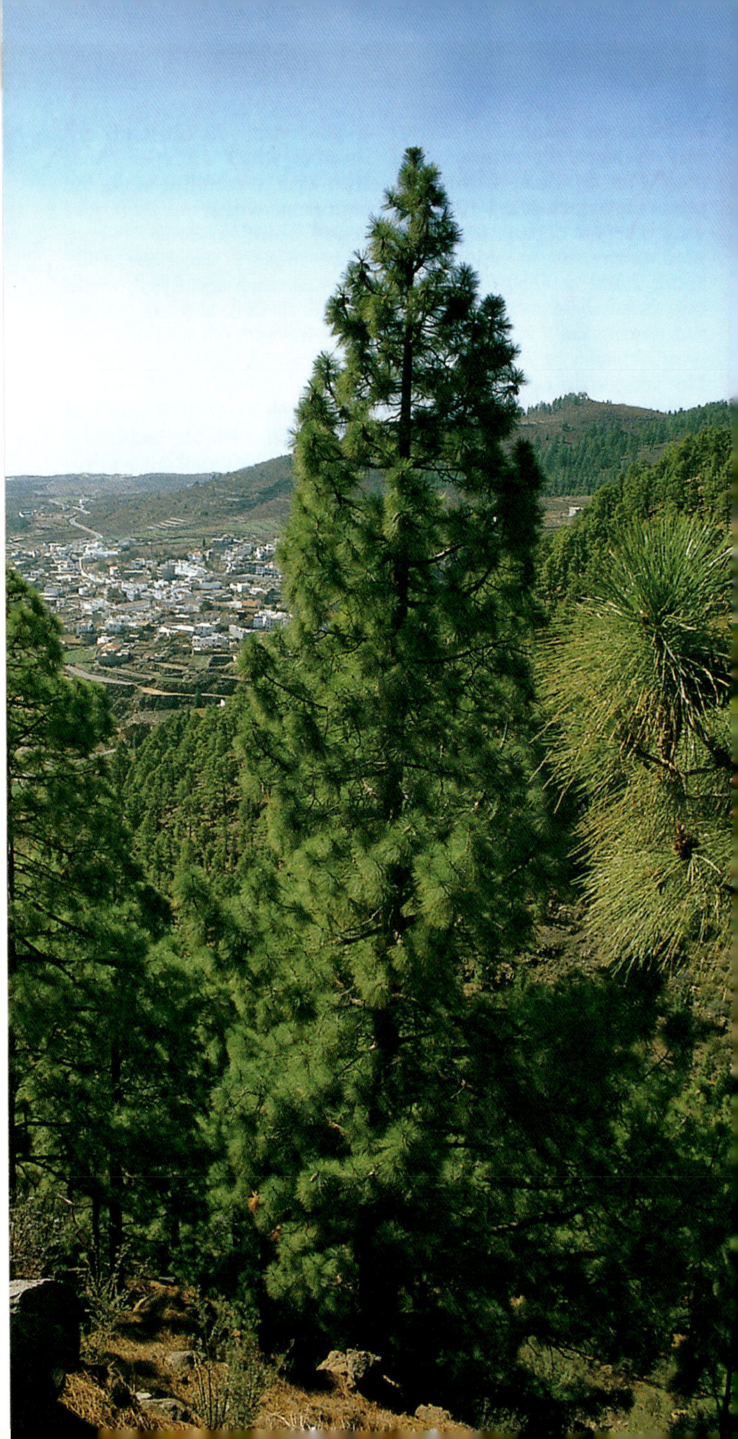

THE SOUTH-EAST COAST

Rugged beauty

*The rural, unspoilt side
of Tenerife lies to the east of the Teide*

This stretch of coastline, running from Santa Cruz to Los Cristianos, is the area least frequented by tourists. If you follow the motorway along the east coast, all you will see is sand, stone and shingle. The monotony of the arid landscape is occasionally relieved by glimpses of the green wooded slopes of the Cumbre Dorsal. If, on the other hand, you follow the old country road, the *carretera*, you will drive through a more fertile region of meadows and cultivated land. The valley of Güímar is especially picturesque and very fertile, and can be regarded as the counterpart of the Orotava valley. The road passes through modest, unspoilt villages whose inhabitants see little of tourists. The majority of people who live here earn their living from farming, fishing and cottage industries. In the bigger towns, such as Arafo and Güímar, there are a number of attractive chalets and holiday homes, but most are owned by mainland Spaniards who stay on Tenerife for the duration of the summer.

GÜÍMAR

(**107/E3–4**) Separated from the Orotava valley by the Cumbre Dorsal, the Güímar valley lies on the eastern side of the mountain ridge. Not as fertile as the Orotava valley, which traps the clouds and their moisture, the Güímar valley has nevertheless been successfully cultivated by its inhabitants who grow a wide variety of fruit and vegetables, including bananas, tomatoes and potatoes. In the middle of the valley lies the town of Güímar (pop. 14,500). On the town square stands the 18th-century church of San Pedro. Next to the mysterious pyramid-shaped burial sites, a visitor centre is being erected. At the time of the Spanish conquest, Güímar was ruled by the *mencey* Añaterve, who converted to Christianity and helped the Spaniards to conquer the island. To the south-west of the town lies the viewpoint of ★ ✿ *Mirador de*

*View of Vilaflor, Tenerife's
highest village, surrounded
by a sparse pine forest*

Don Martín. Below you can see the harbour of Puerto de Güímar and a small sandy beach. There's a typical restaurant here by the name of *Casa Eloy (Category 3)* that offers a wide selection of fish and meat dishes. A good road winds its way up from the town centre through Arafo to the Cumbre Dorsal, finally joining the main Cañadas road.

INFORMATION

Policía Municipal
Tel: 51 01 14

SURROUNDING AREA

Arafo (107/E3)
This small town of 4,100 inhabitants makes a good impression, as most of the houses are not just of bare brick, but are neat. On the outskirts stands an old Canarian pine known as the 'Lord's Pine'. In the central square stands the old church San Juan Degollado, where there is a statue by Luján Pérez. A steep but well-tended asphalt road ascends past small farmsteads all the way to the Cumbre Dorsal and the pine forests. Along the way, the road offers some fine views of the Güímar valley and the Atlantic. On a clear day, the neighbouring island of Gran Canaria is visible.

Arico (111/E2)
The district of Arico (pop. 4,600) consists of three towns – Arico Viejo, Arico El Nuevo and Lomo de Arico, and a few small, scattered settlements. On the coast lies the fishing village Poris de Abona; to the south, on the Punta de Abona, stands a lighthouse. In Arico El Nuevo, there's the interesting 17th-century church of San Juan Bautista, built in Moorish style that reveals Portuguese influence. Many of the whitewashed houses still have old doors and shutters painted in vivid green. For a taste of the local fare, try the *Chinchorro (Category 3)* restaurant in Poris de Abona.

Candelaria (107/F2-3)
★ ✪ The white tower of the basilica in Candelaria is visible from afar. Located on the edge

MARCO POLO SELECTION: THE SOUTH-EAST COAST

1 Mirador de Don Martín
Panorama south-east of Güímar (page 67)

2 Vilaflor
The island's highest village; famous for its lacemakers and healthy climate (page 71)

3 Paisaje Lunar
A fantastic lunar landscape on the edge of the Cañadas (page 70)

4 Candelaria
The basilica of the Candlemas Madonna is a historic place of pilgrimage (page 68)

THE SOUTH-EAST COAST

View over the Marian pilgrimage church of Nuestra Señora de la Candelaria

of a vast square right next to the beach, this church is dedicated to the Candlemas Madonna, Candelaria, the protectoress of the Canary Islands. The statue most venerated by the Canarians is here. According to legend, in pre-Christian times two Guanche goatherds found the statue of Mary washed up on the beach of Chimisay, now El Socorro. Where this dark-hued Madonna came from is a mystery; some say that she came from a boat that had foundered during a storm. Legend also has it that when one of the herdsmen threw a stone at the statue in an attempt to smash it, his arm immediately became paralyzed. The two men decided to take the statue to their king, the *mencey* of Güímar, who decided to place her in a cave. Followers of Diego de Herrera, the ruler of Lanzarote, then stole the statue and put it in a monastery of his island, and soon strange things started to happen. When the servers entered the chapel in the morning, they always found the statue with its face to the wall. Every day they turned it back around, but the next morning the same thing occurred. Naturally, the locals were alarmed by these happenings, which they linked to the theft of the statue, and so it was decided to return it to Tenerife. Thus began the pilgrimages to see the miraculous 'Madonna of the Light'. Every year thousands of Canarians flock to Candelaria on 14 and 15 August to pay homage to the Virgin Mary.

The large *plaza* in front of the church provides the perfect stage for the proceedings. On the seaward side of the square, the statues of ten Guanche kings stand guard.

Candelaria (pop. 10,600) has an attractive old town with whitewashed houses featuring the traditional wooden balcony. Colourful boats in the harbour complete this picturesque scene, complemented by a clean lava beach below the square. New residences and holiday complexes have been built around the town. Some recommended restaurants are: *Casa José (Avda. Generalísimo, 3; Category 3)* and the *Playa Mar (C/. Obispo Pérez Cáceres; Category 3)*. Recommended hotels are: *Tenerife Tour (98 rooms; Avda. Generalísimo, 170; Tel: 50 02 00; Fax: 50 23 63; Category 3)* and *Punta del Rey (437 rooms; Tel: 50 18 99; Fax: 50 00 91; Category 2). Information: Tourist information office CIT, Avda. Generalísimo, Caletillas; Tel: 50 26 83.*

Fasnia (107/E5)

On the road from Güímar to Fasnia you will cross a barren, rocky region where nothing but cacti and coarse weeds grow. At every turn, this winding road offers breathtaking views of the very deep *barrancos* (ravines). To the right and left of the road you also see the many caves that have been carved out of the walls of the soft tufa rock. The impoverished village of Fasnia (pop. 2,500) nestles above a mountain of volcanic ash (202 m/663 feet high), on which the chapel of Nuestra Señora de los Dolores was built. In 1705, the village was almost destroyed by the lava spewing out of the Volcán de Fasnia (2,220 m/7,286 feet above sea level). Luckily, the lava flow came to a stop just before reaching the village. Beneath the settlement is a small, sheltered bay with black lava sand.

Granadilla de Abona (110/C3)

Situated in the heart of a fertile region and thanks to a highly efficient irrigation system, Granadilla is now an important agricultural centre. Vineyards, tomatoes, potatoes and oranges grow all around the town. The village has extended southwards and some smallish industries have moved here. It is the most populated town in southern Tenerife, but it is a working town and there's little of interest for the tourist, apart from a small Baroque church in the centre and a number of squares.

Paisaje Lunar (110/C1-2)

★ About 20 km (12½ miles) away from Vilaflor, hidden away on the edge of the Cañadas, lies the Paisaje Lunar or 'Lunar Landscape'. Above the village, on a right-hand bend near km marker 66, a forest track with the sign of *Palo Blanco* begins. This bumpy 7-km (4½-mile)-long country road passes one or two isolated farmsteads and

THE SOUTH-EAST COAST

ends at the Camp Fuente Madre del Agua. Leave your car here and follow the footpath that leads around the camp. When you reach a tight curve, leave the path and turn left through a shallow gorge. Continue on as far as a narrow ridge that leads uphill and towards a large rock formation ahead. After about 50 m (164 feet), the path forks and you'll see a water pipe leading down to the valley into a *barranco*. Take the uphill route to the right of the water pipe, follow the small gorge to the left and you'll eventually reach a plateau. From here you have a good view of Vilaflor and its terraced fields. Continue on into the forest, where the terrain makes for easier walking. A wide hollow comes into view, where you can admire the bizarre tufa rock formations resembling towers and turrets.

Partial view of Vilaflor, a mountain resort with clean, crisp air

Poris de Abona (111/F2)
This little fishing village lies to the south of Arico, right on the coast. A neat but rather humdrum holiday village has been built on its outskirts. Two small, rocky beaches are suitable for swimming, and sun-worshippers can lie alongside the fishing boats to soak up the rays.

Vilaflor (110/B2-3)
★ Surrounded by terraced fields and pretty pine forests, and at an altitude of 1,400 m (4,595 feet), lies Tenerife's highest settlement, Vilaflor (pop. 1,500). The woodland micro-climate and the clear mountain air are very beneficial for those who suffer from lung disorders. Visitors to Vilaflor will find a quiet, neat little hamlet where time seems to have come to a standstill. There is a small spring-water bottling plant nearby, whose product is sold throughout the island. Just outside the town you can admire two giant pine trees, one 42 m (138 feet), the other 53 m (174 feet) high, each 4 m (13 feet) in diameter! Viewing platforms have been built around the trunks of these wonderful giants. For a truly stunning panorama, follow the signs in Vilaflor that take you to the viewing platform of ❧ *Mirador de San Roque*. The view from here encompasses the surrounding countryside all the way to the coastal spa of El Médano. A small chapel lies hidden amongst the trees.

Vilaflor is renowned for its lace, which can be bought directly from the family-run shops. San Pedro, the church in the upper part of the town, is dedicated to Brother Pedro, the missionary and travelling priest born in Vilaflor who started to build it himself in 1550.

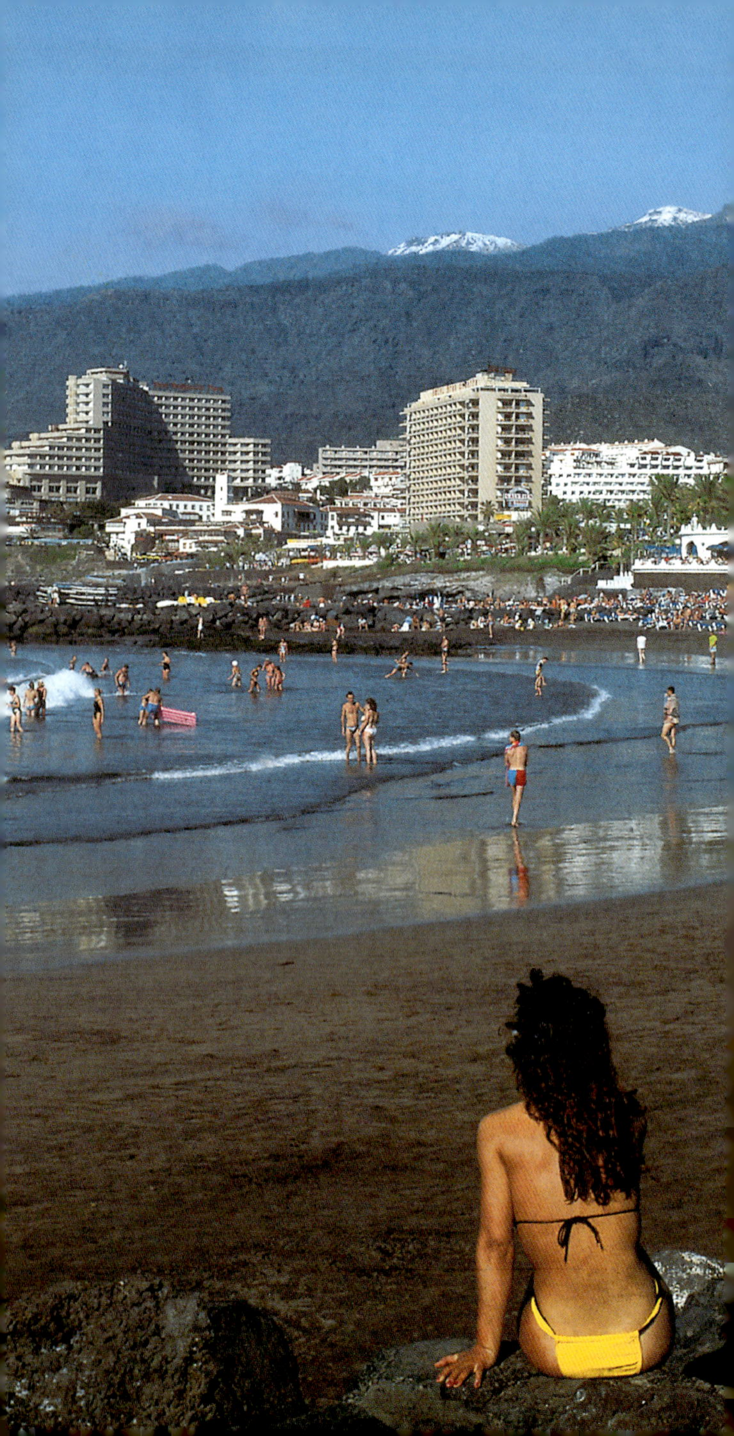

THE SOUTH-WEST COAST · GOMERA · HIERRO

A holiday haven

A haven for beach-lovers and water-sports enthusiasts

The southern tip of the island is dominated by the major holiday resort of Playa de las Américas, a town hewn out of the bare rock and laid out in chequer-board style, joining almost seamlessly with the twin resort of Los Cristianos. If you enjoy scenic views, this part of Tenerife is not for you; the only vegetation here consists of the banana and tomato plantations that slowly give way to the hotels and spas. To compensate, this flat coastal region is ideal for wind surfers and other water-sports fans. If you want to get to know the people and experience something of their everyday life-style, you'll have to go further afield and explore the villages that line the coast: La Caleta, Abama, San Juan, Alcalá, Puerto de Santiago. This stretch of the shore-line is dotted with small beaches and quiet fishing alcoves.

LOS CRISTIANOS

(**109/D5**) This busy town overlooking a broad bay has two faces. As tourism boomed, the former fishing village was literally engulfed by sprawling hotels and apartment blocks, often filled with visitors from northern Europe. The bay is flanked by a promenade and a wide, white sandy beach ideal for swimmers and sunworshippers. At the bay's southern end, a reddish crag juts out into the sea and the bay ends abruptly in front of a desert of scree. Flowers bloom in gardens surrounding the holiday resorts, and young roadside trees offer welcome respite from the blistering sun. A pedestrian zone lined with cafés, restaurants and shops leads to the plaza on the town's outskirts. Narrow streets leading to the harbour

Stark mountains provide the backdrop to the modern tourist mecca of Playa de las Américas

retain some of the atmosphere of the old fishing village. Take the time to seek out a higher vantage point so you can enjoy a splendid view of the harbour. When the ferry or hydrofoil from Gomera arrives, you can watch the port suddenly come to life in anticipation. Light tourist crafts, so-called 'pirate ships', ply the coastline, and a veriety of yachts small and large anchor alongside fishing boats and pedalos. Overlooking the resort, modern terraced houses cling to the volcanic hill of Chayofita. Behind the breakwater, a pretty promenade leads to the Playa de las Américas.

SIGHTS

Cactus Park
This natural parkland holds the world's largest collection of cacti, with over 1,000 species of cactus and desert plant. A brochure is available and gives good information about their characteristics and habitats. Especially interesting is a section called 'Amazonia'; here you can see many colourful hummingbirds, green iguanas and other reptiles, as well as many butterflies and other insects among the tropical flora. You can reach it by leaving the motorway at the Valle San Lorenzo. The entrance to the park is about 200 m (650 feet) higher up (sign posted). All of the surrounding tourist resorts offer a *free bus service* to and from the park. *Daily 9.30 am–6 pm; Admission: 1,250 ptas (for adults) and 700 ptas (for children from 6 to 14 years old)*

Jardines del Atlántico/Bananera
Visitors to this oasis covering 4 hectares (10 acres) can learn about the island's plant life, how the islanders live and how water is collected. Information about departures of the *free buses* from Los Cristianos and Playa de las Américas can be obtained in hotel lobbies and travel agencies. *Admisson: 850 ptas*

Tenerife Zoo – Camel safari
Next to the Cactus Park there is a small zoo that keeps various felines and monkeys; in addition, you can ride on one of the 'ships of the desert'. *Free bus service* from nearby holiday resorts. *Daily 9 am–6 pm; Admission: 400 ptas*

RESTAURANTS

El Cardenal
This is the place for all beef lovers, as steaks are the speciality. Very cosy atmosphere. *Daily 1 pm–4 pm and 7 pm–12 midnight; C/. Juan XXIII; Category 3*

Casa del Mar
☆ Restaurant situated right by the harbour; a wide selection of fresh fish. *Daily from 6 pm; Category 2*

El Sol Chez Jacques
French-style restaurant-bistro. *Daily 1 pm–3pm and 7 pm–11 pm; between C/. General Franco and C/. Juan XXIII; Category 2*

Swiss-Chalet
A restaurant specializing in Swiss dishes, offering 12 different types of fondues. *Daily (except Wed) from 6 pm; Avda. Suecia; Category 1*

THE SOUTH-WEST COAST · GOMERA · HIERRO

SHOPPING

Pedestrian Zone Juan XXIII
This lively area with its countless little shops and boutiques is closed to traffic and makes for an enjoyable shopping spree.

HOTELS

Most of the hotels, apartments and tourist complexes have a three-star rating, but a few luxury hotels have recently been built. Cheaper accommodation in the form of small guesthouses, can be found in the old town, and these are frequented by English, German and Scandinavian tourists.

Gran Hotel Arona
A four-star hotel directly on the bay. *400 rooms; Tel: 75 06 78; Fax: 75 02 43; Category 1*

Marysol
This is an apartment complex with facilities for the disabled; physiotherapy treatments are also available here. About 700 m (230 feet) to the beach. *115 rooms; Tel: 75 05 40; Fax: 79 54 73; Category 2*

Paradise Park
A new apartment-hotel with a very nice garden and plenty of organized activities. *280 rooms; Tel: 79 60 11; Fax: 79 84 59; Category 2*

MARCO POLO SELECTION: THE SOUTH-WEST COAST

1 Las Águilas del Teide
Wildlife park overlooking Los Cristianos, featuring lush tropical flora and birds of prey (page 79)

2 El Médano
Once a little fishing and farming village, this is the only place with a naturally light-coloured sandy beach (page 77)

3 Cueva del Hermano Pedro
A remarkable cave near El Médano (page 78)

4 Barranco del Infierno
Take a walk along this desolate 'devil's gorge' with its 80-m (262-foot)-high waterfall (page 82)

5 Playa de la Arena
A romantic beach in Puerto de Santiago (page 83)

6 Playa de Santiago
Black sandy beach at the foot of the towering cliff of Los Gigantes (page 82)

7 Diving trip
Marvel at the wonders of the deep from the submarine off the Costa del Silencio near Las Galletas (page 77)

8 Nautic
Excellent dining with a view of the Playa de las Américas marina (page 79)

9 El Patio
Top-notch restaurant in Playa de las Américas (page 79)

Princesa Dacil
The biggest hotel in Los Cristianos, with large gardens and a swimming pool. The rooms are comfortable and there's a wide range of entertainment to choose from on the premises. About 500 m (1,640 feet) to the beach. *366 rooms, Camino Penetración; Tel: 79 08 00; Fax: 79 06 58; Category 2*

Tenerife-Sur
Comfortable apartments with restaurant, bar, sauna, squash. 500 m (1,640 feet) away from the beach. *189 rooms; Tel: 79 14 74; Fax: 79 27 74; Category 2*

Pensión La Paloma
A small, family-run guest house that is not far from the harbour. Modest rooms. *Corner C/. Juan XXIII; Tel: 79 01 98*

SPORTS & LEISURE

✱ Water-sports enthusiasts can book boat trips along the coast in the 'Pirate Ship', shark fishing expeditions and even rent pedalos in the harbour. Visitors and tourists need only to go to the beach to hire speedboats, equipment for windsurfing, waterskiing and parasailing as well as other sports accessories.

Karting Club Tenerife
✱ This extensive go cart track is located near the motorway between Los Cristianos and Playa de las Américas. Suitable for families with children.

Deep-sea fishing
✱ For interested anglers, a wide selection of boats are available for hire in the harbour.

ENTERTAINMENT

Dream Palace
✱ This mega-disco features live shows. *Daily from 10 pm; above Los Cristianos, near the Cactus Park*

El Templo
Huge disco resembling an old Egyptian temple; it consists of two large canopies, one for Latin American music, the other for pop. A restaurant completes the ensemble. *Daily 10.30 pm–6 am; Admission: 1,000 ptas (incl. a drink)*

INFORMATION

Oficina de Turismo
At the Centro Cultural, Avda. Penetración; Mon–Fri 9 am-1 pm; Tel: 75 24 92

SURROUNDING AREA

Las Galletas   (110/A-B6)
The Costa del Silencio ('Silent Coast') is the Spanish name for this stretch of coast in the southernmost tip of Tenerife. Behind the coast, there's a wide, flat expanse. The small, attractive fishing village of Las Galletas, near the southern tip, has recently become a busy tourist centre since the opening of *Ten-Bel*, which stands for Tenerife-Belgium, a French-style holiday village in the northern part of town. The complex consists of several living units, mostly two storeys high, and it is surrounded by a tropical garden with several swimming pools, offering all kinds of sports and recreation facilities *(Tel: 78 58 15; Category 2)*. The prosperity of this new development brought to Las Galletas is reflected in the

THE SOUTH-WEST COAST · GOMERA · HIERRO

The harbour of Los Cristianos

many new buildings that have sprung up around its outskirts. The fishing village, now filled with small shops, restaurants and cafés, has blossomed into an attractive and friendly resort. A small promenade runs along the seafront, and a bathing beach where fishing boats anchor lies to the west. This is a good spot for windsurfing; hire boards are available here. ★ *Underwater excursions* aboard the Finnish submarine 'Subtrek' are also offered. There's a free bus service from Playa de las Américas, Los Cristianos and Puerto de la Cruz. To the north-east of Las Galletas, set in the midst of banana plantations and other tropical plants, is the *Nauta* camping and caravan site offering all the usual facilities *(Camping and Caravan-Club Nauta, Las Galletas, Cañada Blanca; Tel: 78 59 71 or 78 51 18)*.

El Médano (111/D5)

★☆ Not long ago, this was a quiet fishing and farming community of 1,000 inhabitants, but in recent years it has been transformed into a major tourist centre. The reason: El Médano boasts the longest and finest beach on the island, almost 3 km (2 miles) long! This spot is also considered a wind surfer's paradise, to the point of having been selected for international wind surfing competitions. The beach extends from both sides of the Montaña Roja, a 171-m (561-foot) volcanic cone. The western side is better for swimming and sunbathing, and windsurfers prefer the eastern side, as the constant on-shore breezes provide the ideal conditions for this popular water sport.

But El Médano isn't only for windsurfers; others appreciate this little resort for its peaceful setting and idyllic, romantic atmosphere. Asthmatics and those who have rheumatic and allergic problems soon discover the healthy climate. In the town centre, behind the square, is a busy beach popular with families and ideally sheltered from the sea breeze by the surrounding hotels. It is said that Magellan himself moored here in 1519 while in the service of the Spanish crown. Despite the influx of tourism, the town has retained something of its original peacefulness; the port is filled predominantly with fishing boats and many of the narrow streets, alleys and houses remain intact. Along the short promenade, around the plaza and in the village, there are many comfortable restaurants and cafés with terraces.

Good accommodation is offered by the family-run hotel *Playa Sur Tenerife*, located close to the beach and with a swimming pool and garden. Cars, bicycles and boards can be hired at the hotel and board transportation is also available. Guests can opt for a room with breakfast or half-board. A windsurfing school is annexed to the hotel *(Tel: 17 60 13 or 17 61 20; Category 2)*. Westwards from the hotel Playa Sur Tenerife is the ★ *Cueva del Hermano Pedro*. To reach this cave, follow the marked path for about 200 m (650 feet) until you reach a turn-off on the right. Continue on this path, and after 500 m (1,600 feet) you'll see it. The Hermano Pedro was a missionary who founded a monastic order in Brazil, which later spread throughout Central America. He was canonized some years ago and twice a year a mass in his honour is celebrated inside the cave. Those who stay in El Médano should pay a visit to the *Avencio*, where seafood is the speciality *(daily from 1 pm; opposite the plaza; Category 2)*.

San Miguel (110/B4)

San Miguel remains an unspoilt village; it lies between Granadilla and the Valle de San Lorenzo. It is known for its lovely flower gardens and orange groves, as well as for Juan Bethancourt Alfonso, a famous physician and historian of the Canary Islands. His birthplace lies to the right of the church. Below San Miguel stands the Castillo San Miguel, a castle replica where medieval jousting contests are re-enacted. Ask a travel agent for further information.

PLAYA DE LAS AMÉRICAS

(109/D4-5) Playa de las Américas is a completely artificial resort that was built on a 5-km (3-mile)-long flat strip along the south-west coast. In the early 1960s, this part of Tenerife was a sandy, stony desert, interrupted by a few banana plantations. When the developers set to work, they decided to relieve what would have been large expanses of concrete with greenery, thus creating large gardens and planting many palm trees along the roadsides. The building of hotels and villas goes on, in an effort to accommodate the ever-growing number of tourists. Swimming and sunbathing here is limited to three fine, but small beaches, so come early. The nightlife, however, is boundless and lively: bars, pubs and discos (especially frequented by the British) are buzzing until the early morning hours. Walkers enjoy the

THE SOUTH-WEST COAST · GOMERA · HIERRO

long promenade that follows the coast round to Los Cristianos. This part of Tenerife is not so much the 'Island of Eternal Spring' as the 'Island of Eternal Summer'.

SIGHTS

Las Águilas del Teide
★ Lush tropical flora and birds of prey are the main attractions of this animal park. These magnificent feathered creatures perform several times a day, while in the evening showmen and magicians are the attraction of the gala dinners. *Free bus service from the major tourist centres. Daily 10 am–6 pm; Admission: 2,000 ptas*

RESTAURANTS

Café-Bar Berlin
German beer pub serving steaks and German food. Good atmosphere. *Daily from 7 pm until the early morning hours; at the ocean promenade below the Hotel Gran Tinerfe; Category 3*

La Karina
Luxurious café-restaurant with a wonderful terrace. *Daily from 10 am; on main street; below the Hotel Sol; Category 2*

Nautic
★ Unusually good food awaits you here. Pretty terrace. *Daily from 12 noon; right on the Puerto Colón marina; Category 2*

Pastas a Go go
Well-run restaurant by the Puerto Colón marina features 99 pasta dishes on the menu, all homemade. Good selection of Italian and Spanish wines. *Daily (except Tues) 12 noon–12 midnight; Puerto Colón shopping centre; Category 2*

El Patio
★ A restaurant and piano bar in the hotel Jardín Tropical; the setting is a typical Canarian patio. Lots of atmosphere and an international menu. *Daily 1 pm–4 pm and 7 pm–12 midnight; by the promenade; Category 1*

SHOPPING

Centro América Shopping
Small specialist shops and market stalls selling beachwear, perfumes, cosmetics and souvenirs. In addition, some restaurants, cafés and bars. *Beside the Hotel Las Palmeras*

City Center
Specialist shops on two floors selling textiles, jewellery, clocks, watches, cameras and embroidery; restaurants and bars. *Between the Los Cardones and La Siesta hotels*

Santiago III
Smart, multi-storeyed shopping centre set in an apartment complex of the same name. All sorts of shops with numerous restaurants and bars. *Open throughout the day*

Shopping Center Bougainville
High-quality shops and a variety of market stalls. Ideal place to buy photographic equipment, electronic goods, leather goods, jewellery, clocks, watches, perfumes and beachwear. You can buy books and magazines at the Bougan-Shop. *Below the Hotel Bougainville*

HOTELS

Playa de las Américas consists mostly of large, modern holiday apartment blocks and villas. The décor in the more luxurious hotels has marble inside and lush grenery outside, generally featuring large swimming pools surrounded by exotic tropical plants.

Gran Hotel Bahía del Duque
Top-notch hotel resembling a Canarian village. Many sports and leisure facilities, suites, conference halls, several restaurants and bars. *362 rooms; Fañabé district; Tel: 71 30 00; Fax: 71 26 16; Category 1*

Gala
New four-star hotel right by the beach. *308 rooms; Tel: 79 46 00; Fax: 79 64 65; Category 2*

Jardín Tropical
Moorish-style hotel set in the middle of a lush, tropical garden. Includes a sports and fitness centre. Restaurant and bar. *427 rooms; San Eugenio district; Tel: 75 01 00 or 79 51 11; Fax: 75 28 44; Category 1*

Pueblo Torviscas
Villas and apartments by the Playa de Torviscas. 'Apart-hotels' also available. *185 rooms; Tel: 79 06 90, Fax: 75 20 51; Category 2*

SPORTS & LEISURE

Swimming
Aguapark Octopus:
This aquatic park at the edge of town features several swimming pools, waterslides and watercourses. This is an aquatic paradise designed specially for children and the young at heart. *Adult admission: 2,000 ptas (children under 11 are free); bus service is available from Puerto de la Cruz, ticket: 2,900 ptas*

Beaches:
The majority of the coastline around Playa de las Américas has lovely white, sandy beaches, interspersed with occasional stretches of dark sand and interrupted only by breakwaters, which help to keep the water calm. The best beaches are probably *Playa de Troya* and *Playa del Bobo*. New beaches are in the area of Fañabé and *Playa del Duque.*

Boat hire
You can hire boats and pedalos at the Puerto Colón marina.

Parasailing
At the Playa de Troya.

Jeep safaris
A jeep safari is by far the best way to explore the island's interior. The dense forest and volcanic terrain are difficult to cross on foot or in an ordinary vehicle or normal hire car, but in a four-wheel drive vehicle a cross-country journey becomes a real adventure. The price for such an outing depends on the route chosen and the meals provided by the operator of the tour. Your hotel should be able to recommend a reputable company. Before making a choice of where to book, it is advisable to make sure that the organization you have selected is fully insured.

THE SOUTH-WEST COAST · GOMERA · HIERRO

Sailing
Boats can be hired in the marina. Be sure to check the condition of the vessel before setting off and verify that all the safety fittings are functioning.

Squash
There are squash courts in the hotels *Europe* and *Conquistador*.

Diving
Enthusiasts can obtain information at the *Diving School Poseidon Nemrod* in the hotel *Las Palmeras* (Tel: 79 09 91), at the *Barracuda Diving and Surfing Club* in the hotel *Paraíso Floral* in Adeje (Tel: 78 07 25) and at the *diving and surfing school* in the hotel *Oasis Paraíso* (Tel: 78 10 51).

Tennis
Almost all hotels have tennis courts; a number of them floodlit. Tennis coaches are sometimes available for private lessons.

Walking
Day-long hikes are organized by the *Innsbruck Alpine Walking School* (enquire at the hotel *Park Club Europe*) as well as by TIMAH-*mountain treks.* (Tel: 71 02 42).

Waterskiing/speed boats
At the Puerto Colón marina and at the *Playa de Troya* beach.

Windsurfing
Boards for hire at the *Playa de Troya* beach.

ENTERTAINMENT

Bananas Garden
Disco pub with terrace in the centre of the Playa de las Américas, opposite the beach. *Daily from 12 noon until the early hours of the morning*

Night-Club Melodies
Friendly nightclub with shows and live music. Join in and dance or just listen. *Daily from 10 pm; in the Poderosa apartment complex*

Memphis
For jazz fans. Programme always changes. *Daily from 10 pm; Lagos de Fañabé; Playa de Torviscas*

Pirámide de Arona
Classical Spanish ballet. *Tues-Sat from 9.30 pm, Sun from 7 pm; Tel: 79 63 60*

Casino
Roulette, blackjack and machines on the ground floor of the hotel *Gran Tinerfe*. Don't forget your passport! *Daily from 8 pm; Admission: 500 ptas*

INFORMATION

Oficinas de Turismo
Urb. Torviscas, opposite the Hotel La Pinta; Daily 9 am–4 pm; Tel: 75 03 66; Fax: 75 20 32
City Center; Daily 9 am–3.30 pm; Tel: 79 76 68

SURROUNDING AREA

Adeje (109/D3)
Although encircled by modern buildings, the centre of Adeje (pop. 2,500) is a quiet spot whose steep main street is lined with whitewashed houses, cafés and laurel trees. Before the conquest, Adeje was the seat of the Guanche king, the *mencey* of Tenerife, and a Guanche shrine used to be at the nearby

Roque del Conde. When the Guanches yielded to the Spaniards, Adeje became the seat of a noble lord, whose family retained control of the town until 1840. The only vestiges of this feudal period are found in the area around the 17–18th-century church Santa Úrsula with houses from the 17th century. The 16th-century Casa Fuerte is situated at the edge of town and is now used as a banana packaging warehouse. Outside the Casa Fuerte stands an ornate cannon. The church contains priceless, 17th-century gobelins, which can be found hanging near the choir stalls. The altarpiece, which was made for the counts of Gomera, features a number of the island's patron saints.

One of Tenerife's most popular destinations for walkers to the north-east of Adeje is the scenic ★ *Barranco del Infierno* (Devil's Gorge) with a dramatic waterfall. It can be reached by taking the path behind the Casa Fuerte and continuing straight ahead until a car park is reached on the lefthand side. There you will find a sign marked *Barranco del Infierno* that points to the recently renovated trail leading into the gorge. The route winds its way along the edge of the *barranco*. At first, the going is quite easy, but the further you walk, the stonier the path becomes, so to avoid injury sturdy shoes are essential. The vegetation becomes denser as you penetrate the gorge. Soon the landmark called *Bailadero de las Brujas* ('Where the witches dance') is reached. The view from here is quite stunning. Eventually, you come to a sharp bend, from which the end of the gorge is visible. Soon you will see the 80-m (262-foot)-high waterfall, which carries water only during the winter months or after a particularly rainy period. Occasionally, after very heavy rains, the route to the *barranco* becomes impassable, as the path is obliterated by the rushing waters; otherwise, it's not an arduous journey, and you don't have to be a highly experienced hiker. Allow four hours for the round trip.

La Caleta (108/C4)
A tiny fishing village, as yet unspoilt by tourism. The sea in this area is clear and calm, but you have to clamber over a number of shoreline rocks to reach it. Recommended restaurants: the *Cala Marín*, which serves fresh fish and seafood *(Category 2)*, and the *Celso (Category 2)*.

Los Gigantes (104/B-C5)
This seaside village owes its name to the truly gigantic 500-m (1,640-foot)-high rocks that rise sharply out of the sea. These cliffs mark the abrupt end of the Teno hills and the beginning of the flat coastal strip. Los Gigantes has been converted into a modern apartment complex, with bungalows and some relatively large hotels. The road winds its way down to the marina and to the adjoining black sand ★*Playa de Santiago* at the foot of the cliffs. Only a few of the village's original buildings remain, and most of these have been converted or

THE SOUTH-WEST COAST · GOMERA · HIERRO

Holiday village in Los Gigantes

renovated. Designed to blend in with the natural surroundings, the *Santiago* with its 382 beds, extensive lawns, large pool and plenty of entertainment is the largest hotel in town. *(Category 1).*

Guía de Isora (105/D6)
This little town lies about 600 m (1,970 feet) above sea level in a barren lava landscape. A good supply of water has helped to create the right conditions for cultivating fruits and vegetables. Much of the surrounding land has been transformed into terraces, where tomatoes and potatoes are grown. Almond trees are also grown here. The church of the Virgen de la Luz, located on the main plaza, was renovated in the 1950s. It's worth a quick visit to see the statue of the Virgin inside, amongst other works. From here you can explore the neighbouring towns of Aripe and Chirche, as well as the Barranco de Tágara.

Puerto de Santiago (104/B-C5)
This fishing village is now surrounded by bungalows and apartment blocks. It is slightly more up-scale than the others, preferring to focus on atmosphere rather than activity, thereby retaining its individual character and attracting a particular clientel. The *Tamaimo Tropical* is an apartment-hotel offering one- and two-bedroom apartments, a restaurant, a bar, two swimming pools, a solarium with jacuzzi and tennis courts *(200 rooms; Tel: 10 06 38; Fax: 10 07 61; Category 2)*. Also recommended is the *Apartamentos Punta Negra* complex by the lava coast (only 14 apartments; *Category 2).*

Below the fishing village lies the romantic bathing beach of ★ *Playa de la Arena*. Above it, a small open area dotted with benches provides a fine view of the beach, the sea and the island of Gomera in the distance. The beach restaurant of *La Sirena*, featuring fish and other grill specialities, is highly recommended. Over supper you can listen to live music and watch the sunset. Further up is a small promenade lined with bars, restaurants, market stalls, a bank and an exchange booth with telephone kiosks.

San Juan (108/B2)
There's always a lively atmosphere in this busy fishing village. The catch is unloaded early in the morning and much of it will end up in the kitchens of nearby restaurants. You can swim by the harbour or off the rocky shoreline, and fish from the breakwater. A popular bar-restaurant is *La Historia de Don José*, where meat and fresh fish are served *(Category 3).*

NEIGHBOURING ISLANDS

Gomera
Tenerife's neighbouring island to the west will soon have its own airport; at the moment it can only be reached by ferry. There are four crossings per day between Los Cristianos and San Sebastián/Gomera; the journey takes 90 minutes.

Gomera covers 378 sq km (146 sq miles) and has 16,000 inhabitants. The interior landscape is marked by numerous *barrancos* or crevices, which widen as they reach the coast. The hilly terrain is punctuated with small villages and hamlets. It may look like a wasteland from a distance, but in fact the interior is verdant and fertile. In the island's centre rises the 1,487-m (4,880-foot)-high Garajonay, to the north lies the *Garajonay national park* (**112-113/B-D2-4**), a jungle of green, where thick forest alternates with dense shrubs. The stunning view from the summit encompasses all of Gomera and the neighbouring islands. On a clear day, the Pico del Teide, some 60 km (37 miles) away, can be seen in the distance. Water is plentiful, and the Canarian palm trees flourish in the lower coastal regions. In the south and east, the vegetation is sparser owing to less rainfall, whereas in the north the soil is rich and fertile thanks to plentiful rainfall and an effective irrigation system.

The inhabitants of Gomera live mainly from agriculture, growing bananas, avocados, mangoes and papayas. Fishing supplements their livelihood, and there are two fish processing factories. The main town is *San Sebastián de la Gomera* (**113/F4**) on the east coast (pop. 5,600). None other than Columbus called here several times to replenish his water supplies on his journeys to the Americas. Also worth a visit is *Hermigua* (**113/D2**), the second-largest settlement on the island. It lies in the northern part of the island, a few kilometres away from the sea and is surrounded by banana plantations. A natural attraction is *Los Órganos* (**112/C1**), on the island's far northern tip; it's a 200-m (656-foot)-wide rock formation consisting of 80-m (263-foot)-high basalt columns, lined up like organ pipes. By far the best place to visit is the *Valle Gran Rey* in the west (**112/A-B3-4**). This lush valley lies between two gorges and its terraced hillsides are covered with palm groves and banana plantations.

In San Sebastián, there is the Parador Nacional *Conde de la Gomera (42 rooms; Tel: 87 11 00; Fax: 87 11 16; Category 1)*. The island's largest hotel is the *Tecina* above Playa de Santiago (**113/D5-6**; *342 rooms; Tel: 89 50 50; Category 1)*, from which you can enjoy a splendid panoramic view. If you are looking for a good place to eat, you will not be disappointed at *La Laguna Grande* restaurant situated in the Garajonay national park (specialities include grilled meat and tuna fish steaks; *Category 2*).

Hierro
Reached by boat from Los Cristianos, Hierro, with its 277 sq km (107 sq mile) area, is the smallest and most southerly of

THE SOUTH-WEST COAST · GOMERA · HIERRO

the Canaries. It has a population of 7,100. The harbour is *Puerto de la Estaca* (**115/F2**). Flying (from Los Rodeos) is not always the fastest or best way to go as the flight is often cancelled because of adverse weather conditions or high winds.

The main town is *Valverde* (pop. 2,000) in the northeast (**115/E-F2**). This is a mountainous island dominated by the Malpaso (1,500 m/4,900 feet), a mountain covered in sparse, green vegetation. Tourism hasn't had much of an impact yet, so farming and forestry are the main sources of income for the small population. There is some attractive scenery, such as *El Golfo* in the north-west, as well as some mysterious prehistorical rock inscriptions. Visitors looking for beaches on the island will be disappointed as there are hardly any.

In the 19th century, a curative spring in the area of Sabinosa (**114/B3**) was discovered. You can stay in the spa of Pozo de la Salud as well as participate in the many cures and physiotherapeutical treatments *(Tel: 55 95 61 or 55 94 65; Fax 55 98 01)*. The island's main hotel is the Parador Nacional *El Hierro* in Valverde *(47 rooms; Tel and Fax: 55 80 36 or 55 80 86; Category 1)*.

The Bay of El Golfo lies at the foot of Hierro's central mountain range on the island's north-west coast

From sea level to the region's highest peaks

These routes are marked in green on the map on the inside front cover and in the Road Atlas beginning on page 100

① FROM PUERTO DE LA CRUZ TO THE NATIONAL PARK – THROUGH ALL CLIMATE ZONES OF THE ISLAND

If you haven't been to Las Cañadas del Teide national park, you don't really know Tenerife. For this 85-km (53-mile)-long drive to Spain's highest peak you will need a full day, as this unforgettable drive takes you through all the island's climatic zones. At the same time, you will enjoy the magnificent views of the northern and southern coasts.

The road from Puerto de la Cruz to the Cañadas starts at *La Orotava (page 36)* and winds through cultivated land where you can see small, modest farmhouses. At an altitude of approx. 1,000 m (3,300 feet), you reach *Aguamansa (page 45)*. All around you'll see well-marked hiking trails; a large, well-kept place for cook-outs has even been built in a crater.

The road continues through dense forests of long-needled pines endemic to the island. Somewhat above the 22-km marker, you'll see on the left-hand side of the road an extraordinary basaltic formation that resembles a giant flower, called *Margarita de Piedra (stone daisy)* by the locals.

As you slowly approach the *Parque Nacional de las Cañadas del Teide (page 63)*, the size and number of trees diminish, until at an altitude of 2,000 m (6,600 feet) the vegetation consists only of broom bushes and small shrubs. At El Portillo, the roads leading from La Orotava and La Laguna meet, and this is where you'll find the *visitor centre* with its interesting exhibits and videos that explain the natural history of the island. Additional brochures inform visitors about the island's geology, flora and fauna, as well as about hiking trails

ROUTES ON TENERIFE

through the Cañadas. Sadly, the tourist cafés higher up, built for the masses of visitors, spoil the view of the natural scenery a bit. Finally, you reach the entrance to the national park. With its 13,571 hectares (33,534 acres), it is Spain's largest. There will hardly be anybody who won't be moved by the breathtaking natural spectacle offered by this high-altitude landscape. The so-called primary crater, a collapsing volcanic basin, measures 12 by 17 km (7½ by 10½ miles); in some parts the rims tower above the crater floor by more than 500 m (1,640 feet). The fantastic kaleidoscope of colours caused by the many different volcanic layers ranges from ochre and dark brown all the way to bright turquoise. Those who hike around the *Montaña Blanca* while ascending the 3,718-m (12,200-foot)-high Teide will experience the full rainbow of colours in all its intensity, and will also be rewarded by running into volcanic bombs, some of them as tall as a person. The locals call them *Huevos del Teide* ('Teide eggs').

On its way to the cableway station, the panoramic road has many vantage points with plaques that explain the odd volcanic formations all around you. At an altitude of approx. 2,300 m (6,600 feet), you reach the bottom station of the *cableway (page 65)* that takes visitors to the *Rambleta* located at the base of the crater (3,600 m/ 11,815 feet). Since tour buses bring throngs of visitors to the cableway station, be advised that, especially during the high season and on weekends, a long queue already starts forming early in the morning. Due to safety precautions the cableway service is not operational when the winds are strong. Nowadays, the crater itself is off-limits to the public to protect its highly sensitive ecosystem. Nevertheless, the *Rambleta* also affords good, clear views. A trail that starts from the Fortaleza in the east and takes you westwards to the Pico Viejo allows for a wonderful panoramic view.

Before returning, an extra trip to 'God's Finger' is well worth your time. This is an extraordinary rock formation that borders the *Llano de Ucanca,* and at one time it was supposedly covered with snow. In front of it you see the recently restored *Parador-hotel* that now boasts four stars and even has a small chapel.

The road downhill takes you back to El Portillo, then continues eastwards on the island's 'crest', the *Cumbre Dorsal.* Soon you'll see the blindingly white buildings of the Izaña astronomical and meteorological observatory. The installation is unfortunately not open to visitors. The winding road eventually reaches the valley, where you can admire the colourful interplay of the different volcanic layers on both sides of the road.

Farther downhill, the forests begin anew; to the right and left you have magnificent views of the northern and southern coasts. Often, as you round a bend in the road you can suddenly be overwhelmed by a 'pea-souper', a cloud pushed by the trade winds towards the northern mountains. You then reach the panoramic plateau of *Las Raíces*, an important spot in modern Spanish history, for this is the spot where in 1936 General Francisco Franco and his followers planned the coup that led to the Spanish Civil War and the eventual collapse of the Spanish Republic.

The panoramic road ends at *La Esperanza*. This is a place where Canarian traditions are still highly valued. Many inns serve the typical dishes accompanied by a good local table wine. Those who prefer something more luxurious can continue their journey and stop at restaurants in *Guamasa* or *Los Naranjeros*.

At the airport of *Los Rodeos* you reach the motorway that takes you back to *Puerto de la Cruz* in approximately half an hour.

② FROM PUERTO DE SANTIAGO TO THE TENO HILLS – A LITTLE ISLAND HISTORY

Apart from offering the famous three (sand, sea, sun), Tenerife also has an impressive luxuriant vegetation that in some cases is only found on the island. The rugged interior with its inaccessible ravines ('barrancos') are an invitation for exploring the area; the small, picturesque villages along the way give you a glimpse of the island's past. To make the most of this journey, you should invest a full day. You start in Puerto de Santiago, on the island's south-west coast and end 100 km (62 miles) later.

The journey's first attraction can be admired right in *Puerto de Santiago (page 83)*, namely the *Acantilado de los Gigantes (page 82)*, a group of rock cliffs that fall 500 m (1,640 feet) straight into the sea. There, protected by the cliffs, you will find a tourist centre with hotels, apartments, countless bungalows and even a marina. The flower-filled gardens and terraces create a lush, unforgettable scenery. Right next to the marina, the small *Playa de Santiago* nestles against the rock faces. At the harbour breakwater, you will find a string of restaurants, cafés and all kinds of small shops right next to one another.

On its way to the high valley *Santiago del Teide*, the road passes through tomato and banana plantations. In this rocky, black landscape you can easily make out the almond trees, and in January their small white blossoms resemble delicate cotton swabs. Grains and grapes are also grown here. Right before you reach the church that resembles a mosque, turn left towards Masca.

The road first takes you to the *Degollada de Cherfe*. When you reach the pass, you'll see a magnificent view of the high valley with the mighty Teide in the background. To the west rise the *Teno hills* with their dark, deep ravines. Far away on the horizon you can make out the islands of Gomera and La Palma.

The road winds its way downhill to *Masca (page 48)*, where tiny peasants' houses cling to the cliffs. Before the new road was built, the only way to reach Masca was by

ROUTES ON TENERIFE

donkey or jeep. Because of its inaccessibility, Masca used to be a pirates' refuge.

Behind the town, the high road to Buenavista del Norte begins. Finished in 1996, this spectacular road takes you to a wild, romantic landscape, where you can literally touch the clouds. Once you reach the high mountain valley of El Palmar you'll find yourself amongst ash and volcanic cones.

Buenavista del Norte (page 45) lies on the coast. On the way to the beach you can stop at several small restaurants offering typical dishes. The jewel of the little town is the church of *Nuestra Señora de los Remedios* that dates back to 1513. Sadly, the valuable treasures it once housed were lost forever when in 1996 the church burned down all the way to its foundations.

A good road continues westwards, winding and tunnelling its way through the massif. It provides truly spectacular views of both sides of the rugged, steep coast before ending at the island's westernmost point, the *lighthouse* at the *Punta de Teno (page 48)*. Ever since it was upgraded, it runs only on solar energy and therefore the lower rooms are no longer used. There's a plan to convert the structure into a mini-hotel or a visitor centre.

From Buenavista to the east, the road passes through sprawling plantations until it reaches *Los Silos (page 49)*. The village square is adorned by a white, pretty pavilion and shaded by laurel trees.

The road continues across a green sea of banana plantations, eventually reaching *Garachico (page 45)*, an attractive, small town famous for being the island's most beautiful. Garachico was the island's commercial centre and main harbour before being largely buried by a disastrous volcanic eruption in 1706. Several manor houses, churches and monasteries bear witness to the town's past wealth. Of interest are what's left of Garachico's former harbour, a castle and several natural swim holes created by the lava.

The landmark of the wine village of *Icod de los Vinos (page 47)* is the 500-year-old *dragon tree*, a first-rate tourist attraction. In the wine pubs in the vicinity you can taste the area's top-notch wines. The little 16th-century village church of San Marcos is also worth a visit. To end your visit you should go to the *Playa de San Marcos*, where you can also savour the fresh fish served by the restaurants.

On the road to the Erjos Pass lies *El Tanque,* also buried by the 1706 eruption and now a place where you can rent camels, allowing you to experience these unique 'ships of the desert'. Judging by the many tour buses and rental cars, this is doubtless a very popular tourist destination.

The road proceeds uphill across fertile fields to the Puerto de Erjos, then a curvy road takes you to *Santiago del Teide.* Below you see the shimmering Atlantic waters and the many whitewashed tourist facilities under the warm, bright, Canarian sun.

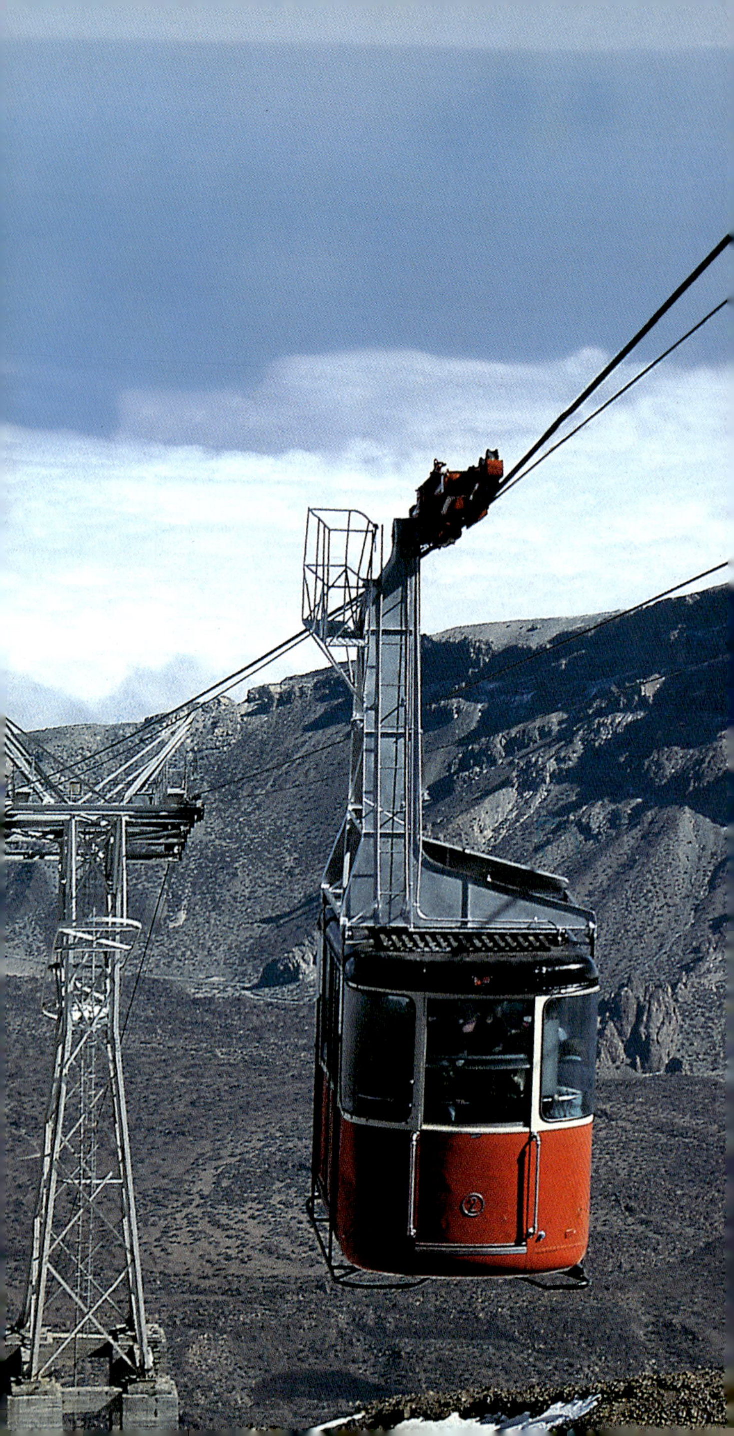

ESSENTIALS

Practical information

Important addresses and useful information for your visit to Tenerife

AIRPORTS

There are two airports in Tenerife: Los Rodeos near Santa Cruz in the north is for inter-island and domestic flights *(Tel: 25 79 40)*, while Reina Sofía just outside El Médano in the south is for international flights *(Tel: 77 00 50)*.

BANKS & MONEY

Banks are open every day from 9 am–2 pm. They usually close on Saturdays during the summer months. Eurocheques are widely accepted and should be made out in pesetas. The maximum amount per cheque is 25,000 ptas. If you want to change cash, the bureau de change rates are generally more favourable, but it is worth enquiring first about charges and commissions, as they vary greatly. It's also possible to change money in travel agencies and at the reception desks of large hotels. Coins come in denominations of 1, 5, 10, 25, 50, 100, 200 and 500 pesetas and there are banknotes of 1,000, 2,000, 5,000 and 10,000 pesetas (see page 120 for current exchange rates).

BEACHES

Most of the light-coloured sandy beaches on Tenerife are concentrated in the south of the island. If you see a red flag flying, it means that it's too dangerous to swim. Not all beaches are supervised so, as a general rule, it's advisable to follow the locals' lead – they know the safest places to swim.

BOAT TRIPS

To Gomera
There are four car ferry sailings per day between Gomera and Los Cristianos. The crossing takes about 90 minutes. Departures from Los Cristianos are at 9 am, 12.30 pm (except Wed), 4 pm and 8 pm and from San Sebastián de la Gomera at 7 am, 10.45 am, 2.15 pm (except Wed) and 6 pm. A bus service is available from Santa Cruz de Tenerife. The single fare for one person is 1,920 ptas and 3,100 ptas for a mid-range saloon car. The 'Barracuda' hydrofoil (20 March

Ten minutes in a cable car is all it takes to reach the top of Pico del Teide

to 15 Sept) takes only 35 minutes and goes on to Valle Gran Rey. Departures from Los Cristianos: 9 am, 12.30 pm, 4 pm and 6 pm; from San Sebastián: 8 am, 10.15 am, 2 pm and 5 pm.

To Gran Canaria
A jetfoil links Santa Cruz de Tenerife with Las Palmas de Gran Canaria. The crossing takes about 80 minutes and costs 5,531 ptas. There is also a jetfoil service to Fuerteventura that operates on Monday, Wednesday and Friday. A car ferry runs between Santa Cruz and Agaete on the west coast of Gran Canaria. There are four sailings every day in both directions and the crossing takes about two hours. The fare for a single journey is 2,876 ptas per person; a medium-sized saloon car costs 9,427 ptas.

BUSES

The local bus company (TITSA) operates a network of services that covers the whole island. Timetables are available from bus stations and TITSA booths. Bus stops are indicated by roadside signs. If you're planning on using the buses frequently, it's worth looking into the 'Bono-Bus' multiple-ticket system, which will save you money. The Santa Cruz bus station is on the Avenida Tres de Mayo (by the motorway exit). The station in Puerto de la Cruz is situated in the Poligono centre (behind the old town). In Playa de las Américas, the buses depart from Pueblo Canario opposite the Gran Tinerife hotel and in Los Cristianos they leave from the central taxi rank.

CAMPING

There is only one official campsite in the south of the island: *Camping Nauta, Cañada Blanca/ Las Galletas; Tel: 78 51 18*.

In Castillo de Himeche, between Guía de Isora and Playa de San Juan, visitors can camp American style at an elevation of 300 m (985 ft). The facility includes a pool and a large communal area (Tel: 86 22 14; mobile phone: 909 14 16 02). If you wish to camp in the National Park, you should seek prior permission from the ICONA environmental protection authorities (*Avda. de Anaga 35, Santa Cruz de Tenerife; Tel: 33 07 01*).

There are no official campsites on Gomera or Hierro.

CAR HIRE/CAR RENTAL

There is a wide range of car rental offices in all the major resorts on Tenerife and at both airports, and vehicles of every size and make are available. It is definitely worth taking the time to compare prices as they vary widely in this competitive business. Rates include unlimited mileage. You will be asked to show your national driver's licence. Alternatively, you can book a hire car prior to your departure. Ask your travel agent for details.

CHEMISTS

A sign with a green cross against a white background indicates a chemist *(farmacia)*. They are usually open from Monday to Friday 9 am–1 pm and 4 pm–7 pm and on Saturday morning until 1 pm. The addresses of emergency chemists (*farmacia de guardia*) are displayed in every chemist shop window.

ESSENTIALS

CONSULATES & EMBASSIES

On the Canary Islands:
United Kingdom
C/. Luis Morote, 6-3°,
Las Palmas de Gran Canaria;
Tel: (928) 26 25 08

United States
C/. Los Martinez Escobar,
3 Oficina 7 C,
Las Palmas de Gran Canaria;
Tel: (928) 27 12 59

in Madrid:
Canadian Embassy
Edificio Goya,
Calle Nunez de Balbao 35,
28001 Madrid;
Tel: (91) 431 43 00;
Fax: (1) 577 98 11

British Embassy
Calle de Fernando el Santo 16,
28010 Madrid;
Tel: (091) 319 02 00;
Fax (1) 700 82 72

United States Embassy
Serrano 75,
28006 Madrid;
Tel: (91) 587 22 00;
Fax: (1) 587 23 03

CREDIT CARDS

In the event of a lost or stolen credit card, contact:

*American Express, Tel: 91/459 90 09
Diners Club, Tel: 91/247 40 00
Eurocard, Tel: 91/435 24 45
Eurocheque,
Tel: 07/49/69/74 09 87
Visa, Tel: 91/435 24 45*

CUSTOMS

From a customs point of view, Tenerife is not part of the EU and therefore some restrictions apply to exported goods. Only 2 litres of wine or 1 litre of spirits, 200 cigarettes or 100 cigarillos or 50 cigars may be taken home.

DOCTORS

All members of EU countries are entitled to free medical treatment. An E111 form (obtainable by British nationals from the social security office) should, in theory, cover treatment expenses, but not prescriptions. It is nevertheless advisable to take out a temporary private medical insurance as this will protect you

---

Safer driving

One habit that local drivers adopt is to let the left arm dangle casually from the car window. It's worth keeping an eye on this arm because when it starts to move, it indicates potential danger. The more agitated the arm, the more hazardous the situation. So don't just watch for the brake lights of the car in front, which are often not easy to make out in the bright sunlight. The important thing is to be ready to brake. Driving behaviour such as this is not part of the Spanish highway code, but it is something that most car drivers adopt and that could prevent you from having an accident or a lot of hassle.

against all eventualities and reduce bureaucratic delays.

EMERGENCY NUMBERS

The National Police *(Policía Nacional)* are responsible for security and traffic.
Tel: 091 (*only in Santa Cruz, La Laguna and Puerto de la Cruz*).

Local police *(Policía Municipal)*:
Santa Cruz de Tenerife, Tel: 092;
Puerto de la Cruz, C/. Santo Domingo, Tel: 38 12 24;
Playa de las Américas, Pueblo Canario, Tel: 76 51 00
Criminal police *(Guardia Civil):*
Tel: 22 11 00

INFORMATION

Useful information for your holiday can be obtained from the Spanish Tourist Office:

In Canada:
34th Floor, 2 Bloor Street West,
Toronto, Ontario MW4 3E2;
Tel: (416) 961 31 31;
Fax: (416) 961 19 92

In the United Kingdom:
22-23 Manchester Square,
London W1M 5AP;
Tel: (0171) 486 80 77;
Fax: (0171) 486 80 34

In the United States:
35th floor, 666 Fifth Avenue,
New York, NY 10103;
Tel: (212) 265 88 22;
Fax: (212) 265 88 64

In Tenerife:
Santa Cruz de Tenerife
C.P.: 38003,
Plaza de España,
s/n - Palacio Insular;
Tel: (922) 23 95 92;
Fax: (922) 23 98 12

Santa Cruz de Tenerife
C.P.: 38610,
Aeropuerto Reina Sofía;
Tel: (922) 77 30 67

NEWSPAPERS

English newspapers usually arrive on Tenerife the day after publication. You can also pick up the *International Herald Tribune* at most book stores and newspaper stands.

PASSPORTS

Nationals of Canada and the USA must have a valid passport in their possession, nationals of EU coun-

---

The eighth Canary

Truth or fiction? The notion of a lost Canary Island has long captured the popular imagination, resulting in epithets as evocative as they are inevitable: this paradise is alleged to have been magical, with crystalline streams, ancient trees, crimson blossoms and tame wildlife. Prosperity reigned and food was abundant. One had only to reach out to pick succulent fruit or to haul in a net miraculously filled with fish. Many sailors claim to have seen it, but say that the island vanished upon their approach. The myth is no doubt rooted in a volcanic phenomenon that rose from the sea, only to be resubmerged.

ESSENTIALS

tries a valid ID card. No visa is required for a stay of up to three months.

PICNIC SITES (ZONAS RECREATIVAS)

❖ Most picnic sites are located in wooded areas and equipped with barbecue grills, benches and sometimes even running water. Many have children's playgrounds too. Firewood is usually provided, often chopped and stored in a pile. Locals frequently picnic in the *chozas*, which are wayside shelters. *Zonas Recreativas* are found in the scenic areas or popular walking regions. In the summer, the Tinerfiños love to leave the towns for the cool shade of the forests and then the picnic sites become overcrowded and barbecue grills are at a premium. The solution is to arrive early.

La Caldera: Coming from La Orotava, this site lies halfway up the hillside on the edge of the Aguamansa woods, near a trout farm. In the wood, near the 16.2 km marker, turn left. This well-equipped picnic site is now only a few minutes away, beside a small pond. The clearing is surrounded by fragrant woodland.

Chanajiga: Leave Puerto de la Cruz for Realejo Alto. Carry on to Cruz Santa and then turn left to Palo Blanco. After about 1.5 km (1 mile), a track leads off to the hamlet of Las Llanadas, and the picnic site is signposted from here.

Las Arenas Negras: Make for Icod de los Vinos on the north coast and then carry on to La Montañeta. Higher up on the left-hand side stands a forest hut. Continue on foot to the picnic site, as the track is very bumpy. After a short climb through a pine wood, you'll find yourself in this magnificent recreational area.

Barranco de Ruiz: This small picnic site with a children's playground lies near the village of San Juan de la Rambla about halfway between Icod and Puerto de la Cruz, on the left-hand side near kilometre marker 48.

Carretera de Chío: Drive through the Cañadas towards the south and then turn left to Chío after the Llano de Ucanca plain. Pass the huge area of lava and then after 10 km (6 miles) turn left to the signposted picnic site and children's playground.

Los Roques: This large picnic site is situated beneath the bizarre Los Roques rock formation opposite the Parador Nacional. A short walk around the rocks starts here.

Las Raíces: Leave La Laguna along the Cumbre Dorsal and just beyond La Esperanza lies a 'historic' picnic site. General Franco once ate his packed lunch here! Turn left off the main road at kilometre marker 9. The site is about a kilometre (½ mile) further on.

Cumbres de Anaga: Drive from Las Mercedes towards the Anaga mountains. After a while you will come across a parallel road that runs to the left to Taganana and to San Andrés on the right. Carry straight on to the Mirador Bailadero, which offers a fine view of the village of Taganana. Follow the road to the hamlets of Lomo de las Bodegas, La Cumbrilla and Chamorga. The picnic site with its splendid views is just ahead.

Las Lajas: Coming from Vilaflor, this picnic site is just beyond the Mirador Pino del Gordo. A

> **In the spirit of Marco Polo**
>
> Marco Polo was the first true world traveller. He travelled with peaceful intentions, forging links between the East and the West. His aim was to discover the world, and explore different cultures and environments without changing or disrupting them. He is an excellent role model for the travellers of today and the future. Wherever we travel we should show respect for other peoples and the natural world.

further 10 km (6 miles) and you will be on the edge of Las Cañadas.

POST

The main post office in Puerto de la Cruz is situated in Calle del Pozo opposite the bus station, while the post office savings bank *(Caja Postal)* is in Calle Béthencourt. In Santa Cruz, the Caja Postal is located by the Plaza de España, in Los Cristianos in Calle Juan XXIII and in Playa de las Américas in Pueblo Canario *(11 am–2 pm)*. Usual opening times: *Monday to Friday, 9 am– 2 pm, Saturday 9 am–1 pm.*

SAILING

For the committed amateur sailor, the Canary Islands have everything. The unbroken, warm, sunny weather means that the sailing season never ends, although the north coast is probably best avoided in winter. With the high mountains inland, the offshore winds can sometimes weaken to just a few infrequent gusts. Wind conditions up to 10 nautical miles from the shore can be quite unfavourable. Between Gomera and Tenerife winds often blow strongly, with speeds of 35 knots not unusual. These weather conditions persist from November to February, when low pressure zones predominate over the archipelago, but the periods of strong winds last from only one to three days. The following harbours are easy to navigate and have good berths: Santa Cruz/Dársena Pesquera; Radazul marina; Candelaria fishing harbour; Puerto de Güímar leisure and fishing port; Poris de Abona fishing harbour; Las Galletas fishing harbour; Los Cristianos leisure harbour and the Puerto Colón marina in Playa de las Américas; Los Gigantes marina; Punta de Teno fishing harbour.

TAXIS

Taxis wait outside hotels and at designated ranks. Fares are charged according to the meter, but for many journeys a fixed fare applies, which can be ascertained before departure. If you use the same taxi for a return journey, you can get a reduced fare. Waiting time is accounted for separately. Taxis are available to tourists for excursions and it is often possible to negotiate a good price.

TELEPHONE

It is cheapest to phone from the light-blue public telephone

ESSENTIALS

booths (Cabina de Teléfono) and these accept most coins; however, long-distance calls are best made using 100 pta coins. Phone cards are available and are convenient for international calls. To telephone abroad, dial 07 first and then wait for the high-pitched dialling tone. Then dial the relevant international code: United Kingdom 44, United States and Canada 1, Ireland 353.

TIME

In winter, the Canary Islands observe Greenwich Mean Time; in summer they switch to British Summer Time.

TIPPING

In hotels and restaurants, service is usually included in the bill unless it is otherwise stated on the menu or elsewhere. However, a supplementary tip of 10 per cent is the norm for hotel staff, waiting staff and taxi-drivers. This extra is discretionary and you are not obliged to pay it if you are not happy with the quality of service or food you received.

VOLTAGE

Electrical appliances run on 220V in large hotels, 110V in the smaller guest houses.

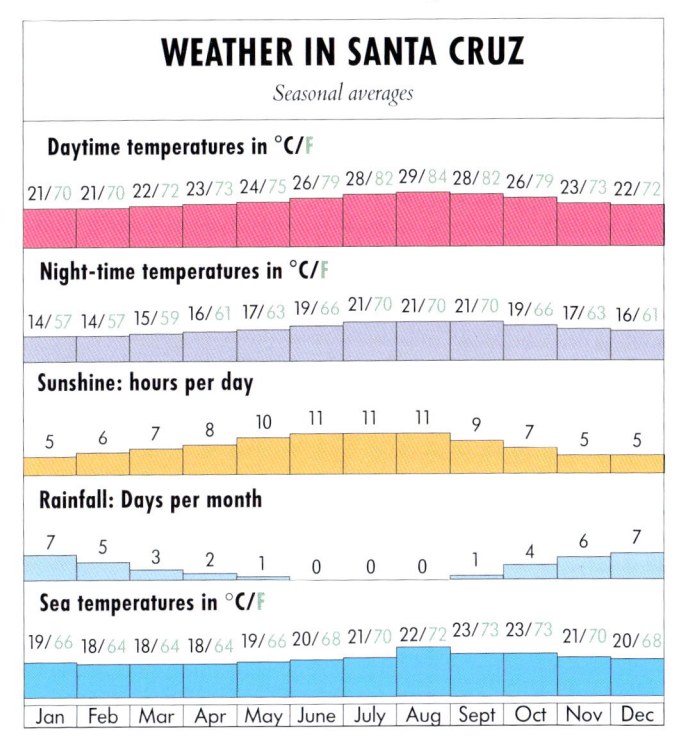

WEATHER IN SANTA CRUZ

Seasonal averages

Daytime temperatures in °C/F

Jan	Feb	Mar	Apr	May	June	July	Aug	Sept	Oct	Nov	Dec
21/70	21/70	22/72	23/73	24/75	26/79	28/82	29/84	28/82	26/79	23/73	22/72

Night-time temperatures in °C/F

Jan	Feb	Mar	Apr	May	June	July	Aug	Sept	Oct	Nov	Dec
14/57	14/57	15/59	16/61	17/63	19/66	21/70	21/70	21/70	19/66	17/63	16/61

Sunshine: hours per day

Jan	Feb	Mar	Apr	May	June	July	Aug	Sept	Oct	Nov	Dec
5	6	7	8	10	11	11	11	9	7	5	5

Rainfall: Days per month

Jan	Feb	Mar	Apr	May	June	July	Aug	Sept	Oct	Nov	Dec
7	5	3	2	1	0	0	0	1	4	6	7

Sea temperatures in °C/F

Jan	Feb	Mar	Apr	May	June	July	Aug	Sept	Oct	Nov	Dec
19/66	18/64	18/64	18/64	19/66	20/68	21/70	22/72	23/73	23/73	21/70	20/68

Do's and don'ts

Some of the traps and pitfalls that await the unwary traveller

Time-share touts

Do not be taken in by the time-share salesmen and women. If someone comes up to you, offers you a draw-ticket and then proclaims in whoops of delight that you have won the jackpot prize, be very wary. These are the sort of ploys that induce gullible holidaymakers to sign up for time-share accommodation deals that they can ill afford. Once an unsuspecting couple have been persuaded to visit a new time-share complex, highly-trained sales-people wear down their victims in such a way that they have little choice but to agree to the purchase of a fixed number of weeks in an apartment. For many people, the realization that they have been conned comes too late.

The carnation trick

If a pretty young woman approaches you on the street, embraces you and presents you with a carnation, beware. These attractive women insist on just one peseta for it. No other coin will do, but while you are rummaging around in your purse or wallet, they will help you in your search, while helping themselves (and with remarkable dexterity), too. And you probably won't realize this until it's too late.

Free bus rides

In the pedestrianized zones and other busy tourist spots, groups of young people spread out amongst the crowds and distribute handbills inviting you to visit one of the island's many attractions. If you are to believe what they say, you can go on one of the excursions at a very cheap price, sometimes for free, and you might even receive a present or win a prize. More often than not, these outings turn into shopping trips where sales personnel with persuasive techniques corner their victims and aggressively sell everyday items such as sheets and saucepans. In this situation it is easy to be forced into buying something you do not in fact want and, what is more, at an extortionate price that easily covers their publicity and transport costs. It is always better to book excursions through a travel agent or else hire a car.

ROAD ATLAS OF TENERIFE

Road Atlas of Tenerife

Plese refer to back cover for an overview of this Road Atlas

99

OCÉANO ATL

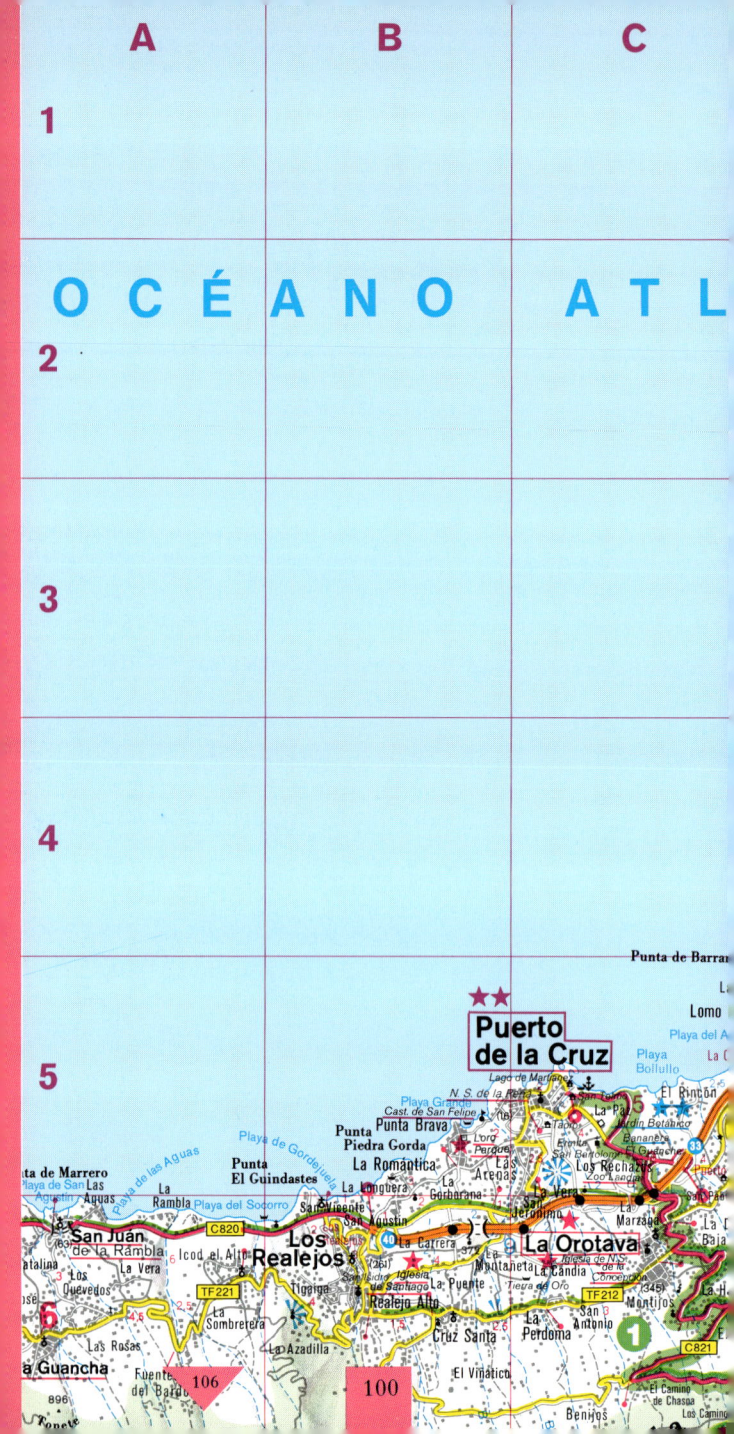

Punta de Barran
Lomo
Playa del A
Puerto de la Cruz
Playa Bollullo
Lago de Martianez
N.S. de la Peña La Paz El Rincón
Playa Grande Jardín Botánico
Cast. de San Felipe Bananera La C
Playa de Gordejuela Punta Brava Loro Parque
Punta Piedra Gorda La Romántica Las Los Rechaz
Playa de las Aguas La Longuera La Gorbarana Arenas
unta de Marrero La Rambla Playa del Socorro San Vicente Jerónimo La Marzaga
Agustin Aguas San Agustín La Baja
San Juan C820 La Carrera **La Orotava** Iglesia de N.S. La H
atalina de la Rambla Icod el Alto **Los Realejos** 40 TF212 de la Concepción
Los La Vera TF221 Iglesia La Puente Tierra de Oro San Montijos
Quevedos La Sombrerera Tigaiga Santiago Realejo Alto La Perdoma Antonio 1 C821
Las Rosas La Azadilla Cruz Santa El Camino
a Guancha Fuente El Viñático de Chasna
del Bardo Benijos Los Camino
896
Tonete 106 100

D
E
F
1
2
3
4
5
6
ANTICO
Playa
Piscinas
Punta Gotera
Punta del Fraile
Caleta del Arco
Milán
TF121
Tejina
la Barranquera
Lomo Rivera
Costa de Valle de Guerra
La Hondura
El Pico
Valle de Guerra
El Cercado
462
Picacho de los Lázaros
El Socorro
Punta del Viento
La Bonifacia
El Pris
TF122
Calle del Vino
Puerto de la Madera
Garimba
El Infierno
El Portezuelo
Mesa del Mar
Punta de la Mesa
San Juan Los Perales
654
Tabares
Casas del Marqués
San José
La Caridad
Guamasa
Cruz Grande
Playa del Camello
C820
Guayonje
Adelantado
Lomo Colorado
Cruz Chiquita
Bahía de la Garañona
Tacoronte
Drago
Campo de Golf
Aeropuerto de Tenerife Norte (Los Rodeos)
El Calvario
(447)
El Cristo
Guía
El Rodeo
El Sauzal
TF5
Los Naranjeros
Punta del Puertito
San Nicolás
Piedras de Asomada
La Cuesta
(322)
Las Casas Altas
El Valle
Ermita de San Simón
Tacoronte
El Cangrejillo
Ortigal de Abajo
Punta Pesquero Alto
La Matanza de Acentejo
El Sauzal
La Montañeta
Agua García
Carril Alto
Ortigal de Arriba
Caleta Salvaje
Cruz de Leandro
Punta de Juan Blas
El Caletón
938
Carboneras
Las Cancelillas
Ravelo
Punta del Sol
Ermita de San Diego
La Breña
Huerta Vicho
(949)
La Matanza de Acentejo
(513)
Madre del Agua
La Esperanza (El Rosario)
Caleta de la Negra
Birmagen
943
Lomo Pelado
Guía
San Antonio
1216
Vista de la Huerta
Sta. Úrsula
Cueva Labrada
Mirador Pico de las Flores
Las Rosas
Alfarera
(591)
La Victoria de Acentejo
Montaña Cabeza de Toro
Preventorio Infantil
Quinta
La Vera
Iglesia
Los Altos
Los Cercados
1500
Las Raíces
(285)
Tosca de Ana María
Las Lagunetas
Las Barreras
Santa Úrsula
Bosque de la Esperanza
Casa Las Señas
Barranco de Maria
Mirador Ortuño
Barranco Hondo
582
Barranco Hondo
La Corujera
Diablillo
Lomo Chupadero
Ovejas
1253
1747
Gaitero
Barranco de Araca
Igueste
C824
Orotava
Las Caletillas
Las Caletas
Playa de
Las Arenitas
Mirador les Cumbres
Bodegas de Chivisaya
Guaya
Araya
Playa de las
Punta Larga
Candelaria
Los Órganos
Las Cuevecitas
23
32
43

101
107

A
B
C
1
2
3
4
5
6
Punta del Hidalgo
Playa de los Troches
Punta Fajana
Punta Tamadite
Punta Poyata
Altagay-Gaby
Punta del Hidalgo
Playa del Arenal
Piscinas Naturales
Chinamada
811
Roque de Taborno
707
Tenejías
Barranco de Taborno
Taborno
Casas de Afur
Tagan
N.S. de
Punta Gotera
Bajamar
Las Montaña
Las Carboneras
Batán de Abajo
Batán de Arriba
El Peladero
755
Moguinal
Roque Negro
Taborno
1024
Las Casas de la Cumbre
TF 114
TF 121
Milán
Tejina
Las Toscas
Tegueste
El Pico
El Cercado
Monte de las Mercedes
Ermita Cruz del Carmen
Mirador Pico del Inglés
Pedro Alvarez
Las Mercedes
Valle Grande
Valle Crispín
462
El Socorro
Lazaros
Español
755
El Palomar
Las Canteras
Ermita
751
Roque de la Fortaleza
Barranco
Valle Vega
Bufadero
El Infierno
El Portezuelo
Ermita de San Diego
Guamasa
Cruz Grande
Hoya del Camello
Las Gavias
La Concepción
LA LAGUNA
Los Campitos
Ramonal
Boca del Valle
10
Valle Seco
C820
Cruz Chiquita
Ermita
Drago
N. S. de la Concepción
Catedral
Ermita
Valle Jiménez
Valle de Tabares
Tahodio
Aeropuerto de Tenerife Norte (Los Rodeos)
Aeropuerto Los Rodeos
El Rodeo
Santo Domingo
San Roque
S. Benito
Vía Ronda/P. Anchieta
Vivero del Distrito Forestal
La Laguna
Valle de Colín
449
La Higuerita
La Cuesta
Parque Municipal
Plaza de Toros
Barrio de la
Club Náutico
Cast. de Paso Alto
Puerto
San Francisco
Museo Arqueológico
Catedral de la Cor
Asomada
Ortigal de Abajo
C824
Guajara
Las Chumberas
Los Baldíos
San Bartolomé de Geneto
Vista Bella
C820
Barriada del General García Escámez
Sanatorio de Ofra
Sofia
SAN
DE TEN
Punta Maragallo
Cementerio
Barrio de Chamberí
de Arriba
938
Carboneras
Las Galeras
San Miguel de Geneto
Las Chumberas
Hospital
Taco
Taco
Taco
Mayorazgo
Hoya Fría
Birmagen
943
Lomo Pelado
Llano del Moro
Sobradillo
Barranco Grande
TF2
Hoya Fría
Playa del Muerto
Las Rosas
El Tablero
Santa María del Mar
Santa María del Mar
Punta de la Encendida
Preventorio Infantil
Las Barreras
Machado
El Pilar
San Isidro
Punta Pachona
La Suerte del Espino
Nuestra Señora del Rosario
C822
Playa Berruguete
582
Barranco Hondo
Tabaiba
TF1
Tabaiba
Radazul
Playa de la Nea
Urbanización Radazul
Punta de Guadamojete
Barranco Hondo
23
Punta del Morro
Igueste
Las Caletillas
Las Caletillas
Playa de las Caletas
Las Arenitas
Playa de las Arenas
Punta Larga
Candelaria
Candelaria

107

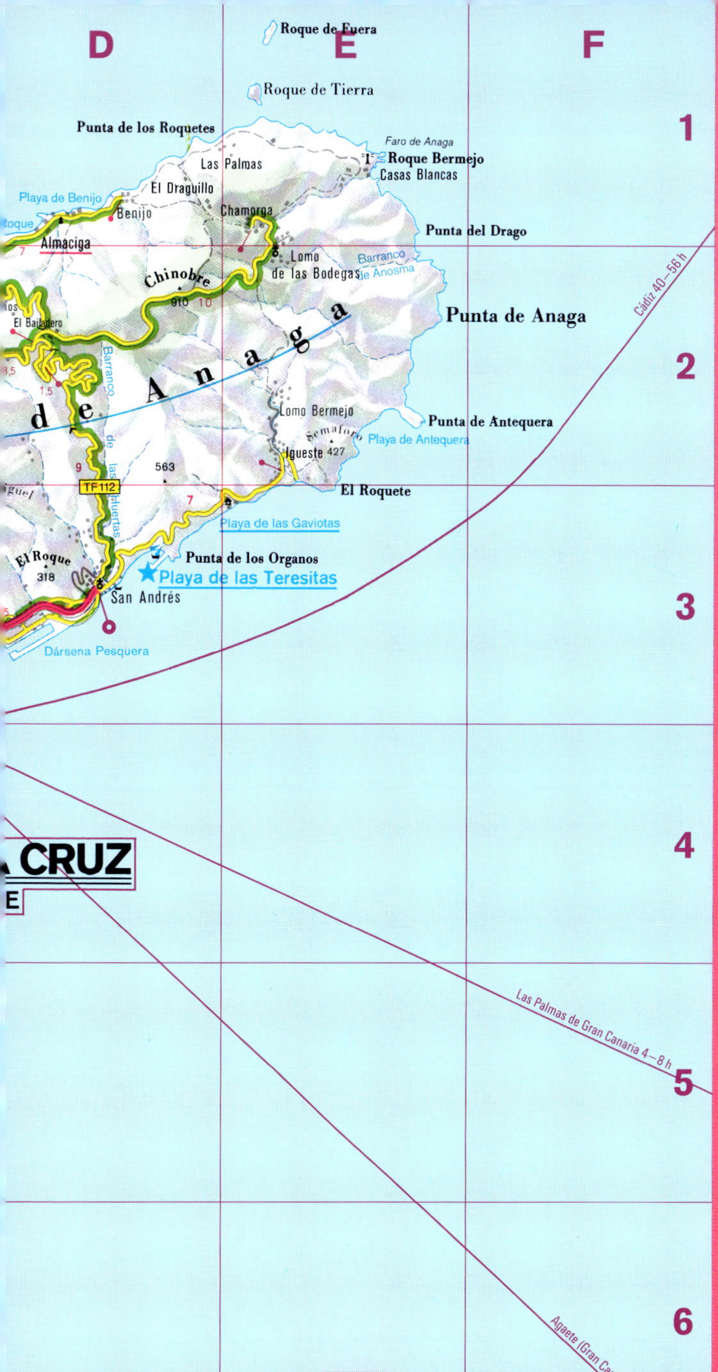
D
E
F
1
2
3
4
5
6
Roque de Fuera
Roque de Tierra
Punta de los Roquetes
Faro de Anaga
Roque Bermejo
Casas Blancas
Las Palmas
El Draguillo
Playa de Benijo
Benijo
Chamorga
Almáciga
Punta del Drago
Lomo
de las Bodegas
Barranco
de Anosma
Chinobre
910
10
El Bailadero
Punta de Anaga
Cádiz 40–56 h
de Anaga
Barranco de las Huertas
Lomo Bermejo
Semáforo
Punta de Antequera
Playa de Antequera
Igueste
427
563
9
TF112
7
El Roquete
Playa de las Gaviotas
Punta de los Organos
Playa de las Teresitas
El Roque
318
San Andrés
Dársena Pesquera
CRUZ
Las Palmas de Gran Canaria 4–8 h
Agaete (Gran Canaria) 2 h

A B C

1
OCÉANO A

2
Punta de la Laja — Punta del Casado
Buenavista — La Costa — Playa del Puertito
Punta Negra — del Norte — San — San José — La Caleta
Punta del Fraile — Bernardo — Los Silos — TF 142
Punta Morro del Diablo — El Pozo
Punta de la Gaviota — Mirador — La Cuesta — Tierra
Punta — de Don Pompeyo — Casa Blanca — del Tri
del Ancón — Las Casas — **Macizo** — 746 — El Lomo Morin
Caleta de Bastián — 657 — Contera de Talavera — Las Cuevas Negras

3
★ Punta de Teno — Faro de Teno — El — Portela Baja
Punta Diente de Ajo — Teno Alto — Erjos — Ermita de San
Punta de la Hábiga — Las Portelas — Puerto de Erjos — Herjos del Tanque — 27
Carrizal Bajo — de — 1117
Carrizal Alto

4
Playa del Carrizal — **Teno** — Valle de Ar
La Vica
Puntilla Los Abades — 915 ★★ Masca — Santiago del Teide
Playa de Juán López — Pico de Yeye — Casas de Araza — Las Manc
Punta de la Galera — Barranco de Masca — 1131
Finca de Guergues — Roque Blanco — 942 — El Retamer

5
Playa de Barranco Seco — El Malpais
Punta de B.co Seco — Taimaimo — (903) Arguayo
La Canalita
★ Acantilado de los Gigantes — C820
La Punta — 4,5
Los Gigantes — Puerto de Santiago — Chio

6
Playa de la Arena
Punta de Barbero
El Costado
Callao Chico — Los Pajares
Punta Blanca — Las Tabladas
Punta de Alcalá — (84) — TF
Alcalá — Charquetas

▼ 108   104

ATLÁNTICO

Punta de las Fajana
Punta de Juan Centellas
Playa de Santo Domingo
Playa Salvaje Punta de Marrero
Playa de San Agustín Las Aguas
Ermita de Santo Domingo Agua Grande
15
San Juan de la Ran
oque de Garachico Playa de San Marcos
Punta de Riquer Playa Moreno
San Marcos
Santa Catalina Los Quevedos
2
Caleta Punta de las Coladas La Costa La
Castillo de Playa de las Aguas Las Cañas La Centinela San José
Buen Paso TF 222
Sta Bárbara Hoya Nadia El Piñalete Las Rosas
El Molino La Mancha
Garachico El Guincho C820 La Guancha
La Vega El Lomo Blanco Llanito de Perea Ermita La Cruz del Franco 896
Icod de los Vinos
San Juan del Reparo El Amparo Barranco Topere
(462) Ermita de Bermebe Pino de Valoy Hoya de Padilla
La Culata La Vega Cueva de Viento Cueva del Viento
rrio Nuevo Lomo Alto El Mortero
La Hoya del Toro La Montañeta 1124 El Amparo Hoya de Redondo 3
Casa Canales Los Marque
Las Abiertas
n José de Las Hiedras la Galera
s Llanos

El Volcán Negro Parque
1626 Nacional Cueva de los Caza
nquis del Teide
1526
Montaña del Estrecho 4
Laderas del

1745
Montaña de Abeque 3718 Cueva Hielo
1764 Pico de Te
29 1805 Mña Reventada Pico Viejo
2235 2994 3135 **
25 Cuevas Negras 2909
Las Narices del Teide 5
2000 Puerto de Cañad
Mirador de Chio

2265 Las
Montañas del Cedro C823 ★★
C823 2114 Llano de Uca
guergue Boca del Tauce Los Re
Aripe Chirche 2195 2090 7 6
Iglesia de la Virgen de la Luz Mña Gangarro 2534
sora (612)
C822 El Jaral
Acojeja
2.5
105 109
Las Fuentes

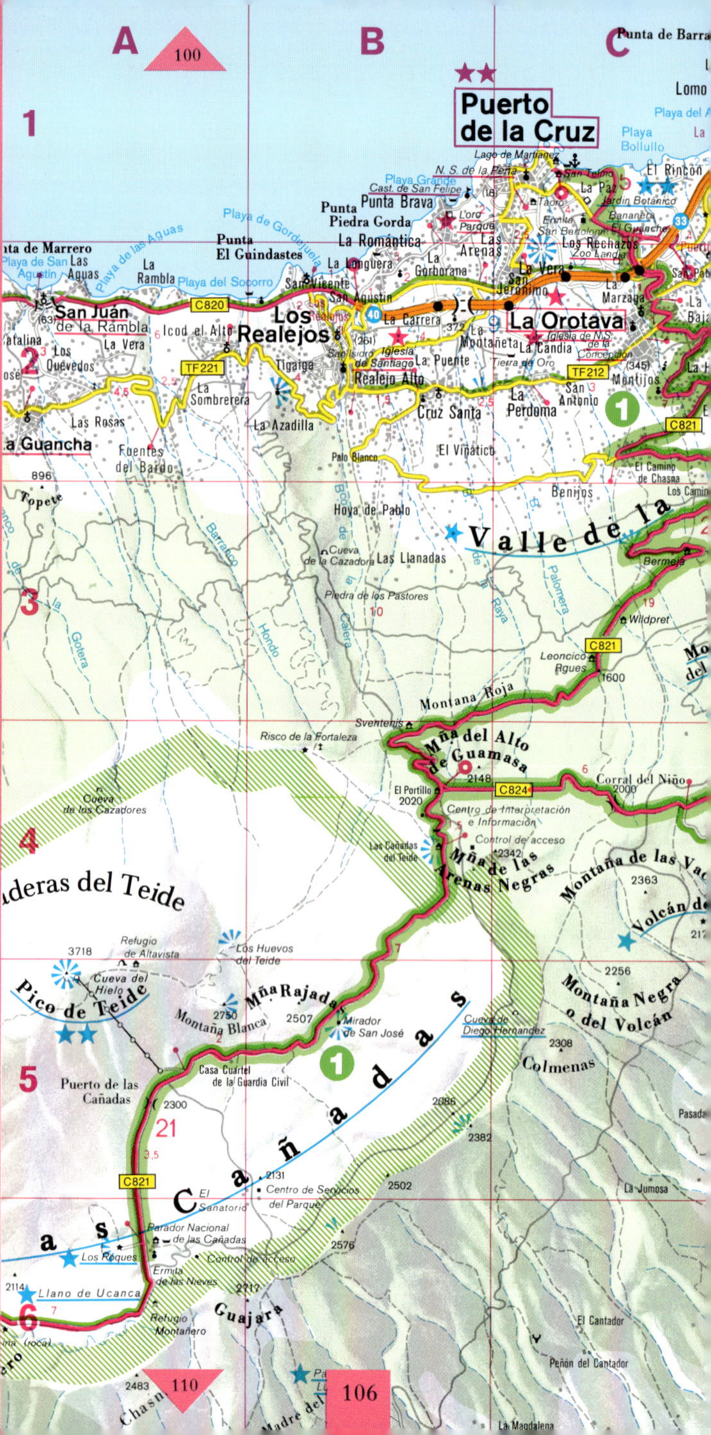
A
B
C
100
1
2
3
4
5
6
Punta de Barra
Lomo
Puerto de la Cruz
Playa del
Playa Bollullo
Lago de Martiánez
N. S. de la Peña
San Telmo
El Rincón
Playa Grande
Cast. de San Felipe
La Paz
Jardín Botánico
Punta Brava
Punta Piedra Gorda
Loro Parque
Taoro
Bananera El Guanche
Ermita San Bartolomé
Los Rechazos
Zoo Landia
Playa de Gordejuela
La Romántica
Las Arenas
Punta El Guindastes
La Longuera
La Gorborana
La Vera
San Jerónimo
La Marzagá
La Baja
Playa de las Aguas
nta de Marrero
Playa de San Agustín
Las Aguas
La Rambla
Playa del Socorro
San Vicente
San Agustín
C820
San Juan de la Rambla
Icod el Alto
Los Realejos
La Carrera
La Montañeta
La Orotava
La Candia
Iglesia de N.S. de la Concepción
Catalina
Los Quevedos
La Vera
San Isidro
Iglesia de Santiago
La Puente
Tierra de Oro
TF221
Tigaiga
Realejo Alto
TF212
Montijos
La Sombrerera
La Azadilla
Cruz Santa
La Perdoma
San Antonio
Las Rosas
La Guancha
Fuentes del Bardo
Palo Blanco
El Vinático
C821
El Camino de Chasna
896
Topete
Benijos
Los Caminos
Hoya de Pablo
Valle de la
Cueva de la Cazadora
Las Llanadas
Bermeja
Barranco Hondo
Bco. de la Catera
Piedra de los Pastores
de la Gotera
Palomera
Wildpret
Leoncico Rgues
C821
1600
Montaña Roja
Sventenis
Risco de la Fortaleza
Mña del Alto de Guamasa
2148
El Portillo
2020
C824
Corral del Niño
2000
Cueva de los Cazadores
Centro de Interpretación e Información
Control de acceso
2342
Las Cañadas del Teide
Mña de las Arenas Negras
Montaña de las Vac
2363
Volcán de
deras del Teide
Refugio de Altavista
3718
Los Huevos del Teide
2256
Cueva del Hielo
Pico de Teide
2750
Montaña Blanca
Mña Rajada
2507
Mirador de San José
Cueva de Diego Hernández
Montaña Negra o del Volcán
2308
Colmenas
Casa Cuartel de la Guardia Civil
Puerto de las Cañadas
2300
21
2086
2382
Pasada
C821
2131
Centro de Servicios del Parque
2502
La Jumosa
Las Cañadas
El Sanatorio
Parador Nacional de las Cañadas
Los Roques
Control de acceso
2576
2114
Llano de Ucanca
Ermita de las Nieves
2717
Guajara
Refugio Montañero
El Cantador
(roca)
Peñón del Cantador
110
2483
Chasna
Madre del
La Magdalena

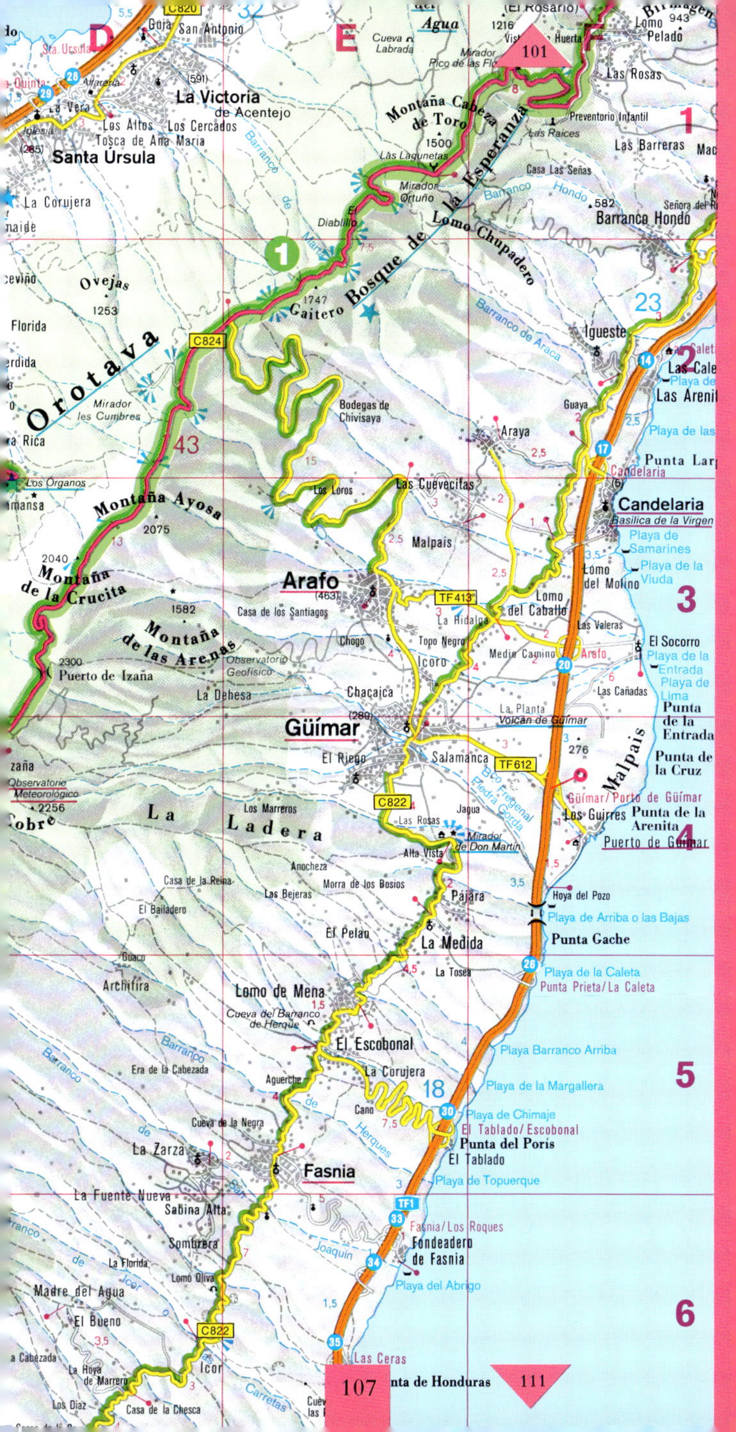

A B C

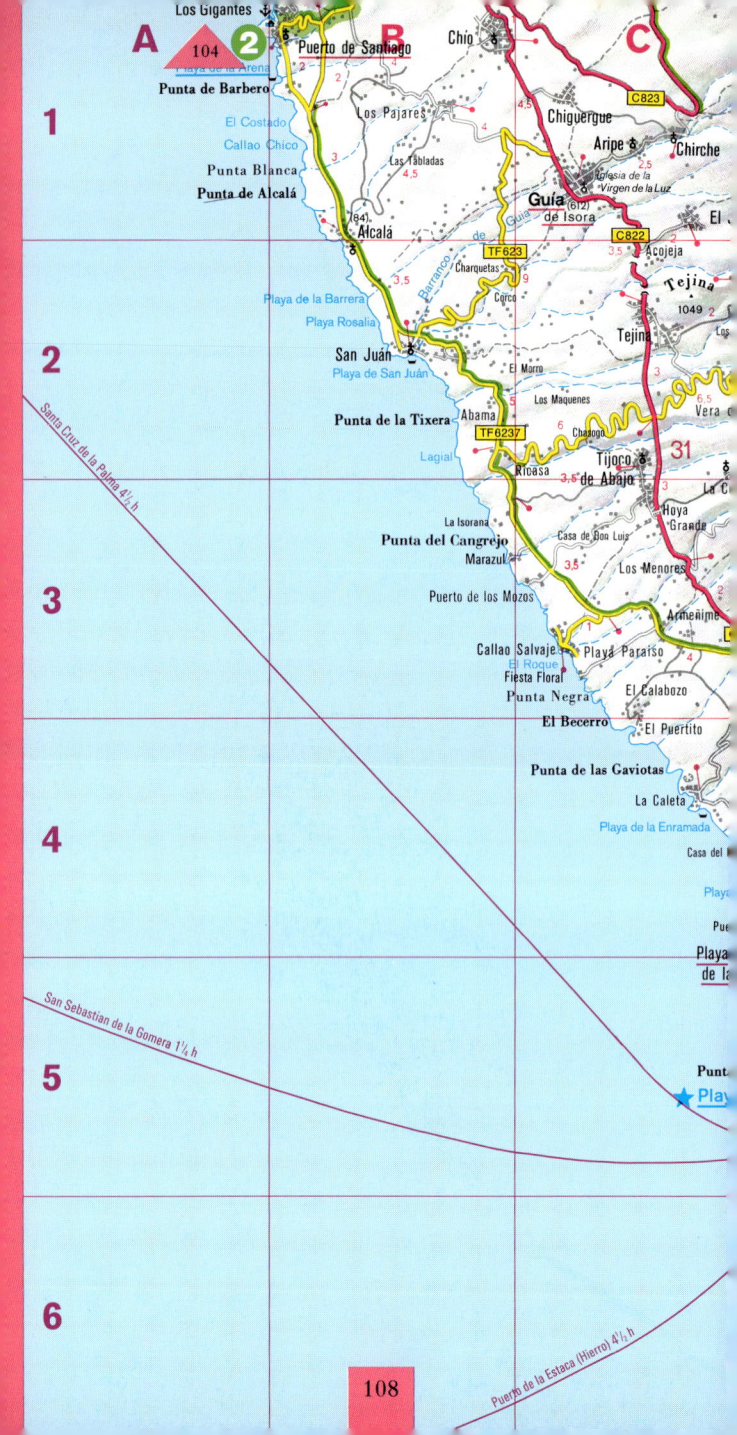

1

Los Gigantes
Punta de Barbero
Playa de la Arena
El Costado
Callao Chico
Punta Blanca
Punta de Alcalá
Puerto de Santiago
Los Pajares
Las Tabladas
Chio
Chiguergue
Aripe
Iglesia de la Virgen de la Luz
Chirche
C823
Alcalá
(84)
TF 623
C822
Guía de Isora
Acojeja
El

2

Barranco
Charquetas
Corco
Playa de la Barrera
Playa Rosalía
San Juán
Playa de San Juán
Punta de la Tixera
Abama
El Morro
Los Maqueños
TF 6237
Chasogo
Ricasa
Tijoco de Abajo
Tejina
1049
Tejina
Vera
31
La C
Hoya Grande
Santa Cruz de la Palma 4½ h

3

Lagial
La Isorana
Punta del Cangrejo
Marazul
Puerto de los Mozos
Callao Salvaje
El Roque
Fiesta Floral
Punta Negra
El Becerro
Casa de Don Luis
Los Menores
Armeñime
Playa Paraíso
El Calabozo
El Puertito

4

Punta de las Gaviotas
La Caleta
Playa de la Enramada
Casa del
Playa
Pue
Playa de la

San Sebastian de la Gomera 1¼ h

5

Punt
Playa

6

Puerto de la Estaca (Hierro) 4½ h

104 2
108

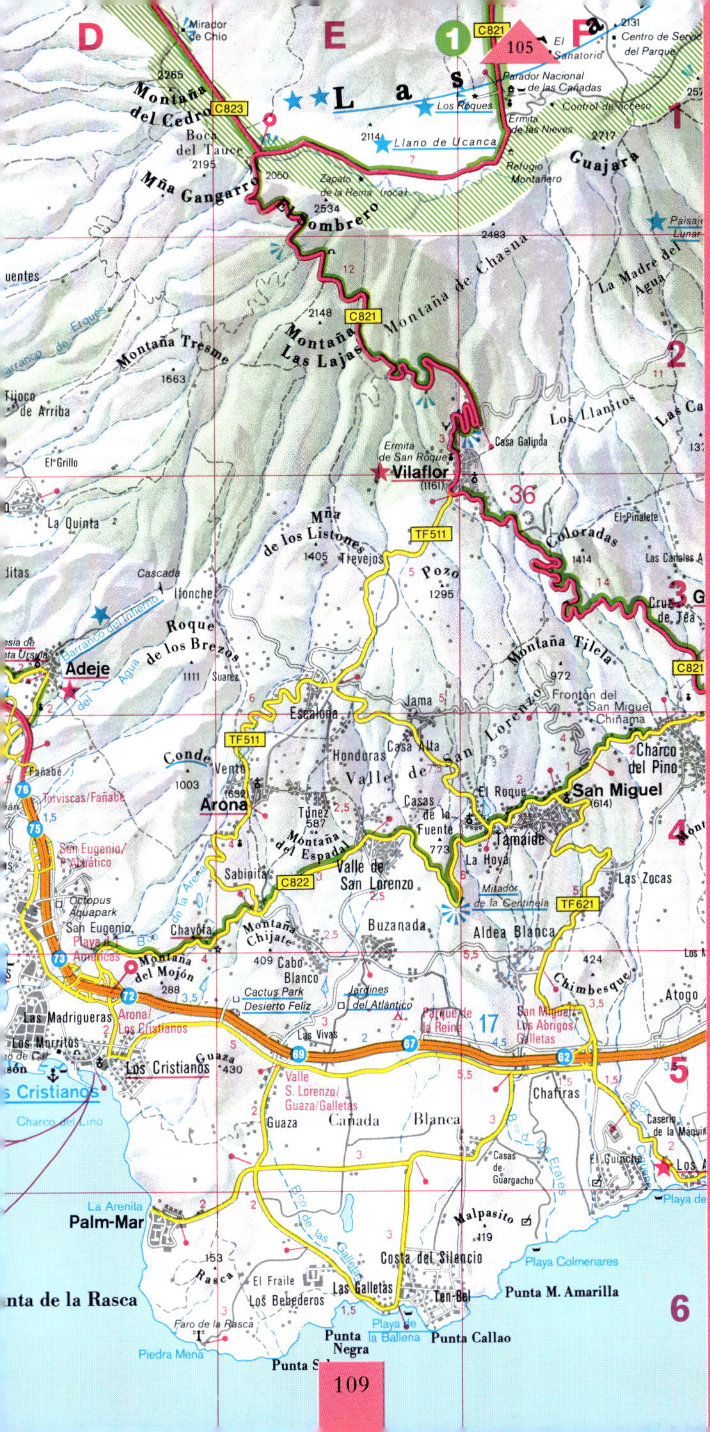

D
E
F
1
105
C821
C823
C822
TF511
TF621
Las Cañadas
Mirador de Chio
Montaña del Cedro
Boca del Tauce
Mña Gangarro
El Sombrero
Parador Nacional de las Cañadas
Los Roques
Llano de Ucanca
Ermita de las Nieves
Refugio Montañero
Zapato de la Reina (roca)
Guajara
El Sanatorio
Centro de Servicio del Parque
Control de acceso
Paisaje Lunar
La Madre del Agua
Montaña de Chasna
Montaña Las Lajas
Montaña Tresme
Barranco de Erques
Tijoco de Arriba
El Grillo
La Quinta
Vilaflor
Ermita de San Roque
Casa Galinda
Los Llanitos
El Pinalete
Coloradas
Las Canales
Cruz de Tea
Mña de los Listones
Trevejos
Pozo
Cascada
Ifonche
Barranco del Infierno
Roque de los Brezos
Adeje
Suarez
Montaña Tilela
Frontón del San Miguel
Chiñama
Jama
Escalona
Conde
Vento
Arona
Honduras
Casa Alta
Valle de San Lorenzo
Charco del Pino
San Miguel
El Roque
Túnez
Casas de la Fuente
Tamaide
La Hoya
Montaña del Espadal
Sabinita
Las Zocas
Mirador de la Centinela
Aldea Blanca
Buzanada
Chayofa
Montaña Chijate
Cabo Blanco
Chimbesque
Atogo
Fañabé
Torviscas/Fañabé
San Eugenio/Aquático
Octopus Aquapark
San Eugenio
Playa de las Américas
Montaña del Mojón
Cactus Park
Desierto Feliz
Jardines del Atlántico
Parque de la Reina
San Miguel/Los Abrigos/Galletas
Las Madrigueras
Arona/Los Cristianos
Los Morritos
Las Vivas
Los Cristianos
Guaza
Charco del Lino
Valle S. Lorenzo/Guaza/Galletas
Chafiras
Caserío de la Máquina
Cañada Blanca
Casas de Guargacho
El Guincho
Los Abrigos
Playa de
La Arenita
Palm-Mar
Malpasito
Costa del Silencio
Playa Colmenares
Rasca
El Fraile
Los Bebederos
Las Galletas
Ten-Bel
Punta M. Amarilla
Punta de la Rasca
Faro de la Rasca
Playa de la Ballena
Punta Callao
Punta Negra
Piedra Mena
17
36
2
3
4
5
6

106
A
B
C
1
2
3
4
5
6
36
17
110
Mirador de Chio
2265
Montaña del Cedro
C823
C821
Las Cañadas
El Sanatorio
2131
Centro de Servicios del Parque
2502
Parador Nacional de las Cañadas
Los Roques
Control de acceso
2576
Ermita de las Nieves
2712
Boca del Tauce
2195
2114
Llano de Ucanca
Guajara
Refugio Montañero
2050
Mña Gangarro
Zapato de la Reina (roca)
2534
El Sombrero
2483
Paisaje Lunar
La Madre del Agua
Montaña de Chasna
2148
Montaña Las Lajas
Montaña Tresme
1663
Los Llanitos
Las Calderas
1371
Ermita de San Roque
Casa Galinda
Vilaflor
(1161)
Mña de los Listones
1405
Trevejos
TF511
El Pinalete
Coloradas
1414
Las Canales Altas
La Higue
Cascada
Ifonche
Pozo
1295
Cruz de Tea
Granadilla de Abona
Los Barr
Roque de los Brezos
1111
Suarez
Montaña Tilela
972
(654)
Vicacaro
Escalona
Jama
Fronton del San Miguel
Chiñama
El Draguito
Conde
1003
Vento
Honduras
Casa Alta
Valle de San Lorenzo
Charco del Pino
El Salto
Arona
(632)
Túnez
587
Casas de la Fuente
El Roque
San Miguel
(614)
Capellania
Montaña del Espadal
773
Tamaide
La Hoya
Montaña Gorda
646
Hoya d
Yaco
Sabinita
C822
Valle de San Lorenzo
Mirador de la Centinela
TF621
Las Zocas
Barranco de
Chayofa
Montaña Chijate
Buzanada
Aldea Blanca
Montaña del Mojón
288
409
Cabo Blanco
424
Los Molinos
Casablanca
Chimbesque
Atogo
Cactus Park
Desierto Feliz
Jardines del Atlántico
Parque de la Reina
San Miguel/ Los Abrigos/ Galletas
Aeropuerto del Sur
Cristianos
Las Vivas
Guaza
430
Los Cristianos
Valle S. Lorenzo/ Guaza/Galletas
Chafiras
Guaza
Cañada
Blanca
Caserío de la Maquina
Aeropuerto Tenerife S (Reina Sofía)
Casas de Guargacho
El Guincho
Los Abrigos
El Confital
Playa de San Blas
Playa de la
Malpasito
119
153
Rasca
Costa del Silencio
Playa Colmenares
El Fraile
Los Bebederos
Las Galletas
Ten-Bel
Punta M. Amarilla
Faro de la Rasca
Playa de la Ballena
Punta Callao
Piedra Mena
Punta Negra
Punta Salema

D
E
F
1
2
3
4
5
6
107
17
Fasnia
La Zarza
La Jumosa
La Fuente Nueva
Sabina Alta
Sombrera
La Florida
Lomo Oliva
Madre del Agua
El Bueno
El Cantador
Peñón del Cantador
La Cabezada
La Hoya de Marrero
Icor
C822
TF1
Fasnia/Los Roq
Fondeadero de Fasnia
Playa del Abrigo
Joaquín
Las Ceras
Punta de Honduras
Los Díaz
Casa de la Chesca
Casas de la Cera
Cuevas de las Ricas
Carretas
Playa de las Ceras
Punta del Rincón
Montaña Magua
Degollada
Arico Viejo
Arico
El Arrecife
Las Silletas
La Sabinita
Los Gavitanes
Arico El Nuevo
Villa de Arico
Casas del Viso
La Cancela
Arico/ Poris de Abona
Playa de la Caleta
Punta la Ternera
Poris de Abona
Puerto de Abona
La Cisnera
Lomo de Arico
Playa Grande
Punta de los Requetés
Casas El Faro
El Viento
El Frontón
Casas San Juán
Reverón
Montaña Centinela
Sanatorio de Abona
Abades
Las Rosas
El Rio
Punta de Cueva Nueva
Playa de los Abrigos
Punta de Abades
Chimiche
Salto del Roque
Ensenada de Abades
Punta de los Jureles
La Jaca
P.I.R.S. Tajao
Ensenada Piedra de la Sal
Punta del Sordo
Playa de Cayado Hondo
San Miguel de Tajao
El Vallito
Chimiche/ El Rio
Cueva Honda
Barranco del Rio
Pol. Industrial Granadilla
Playa del Rio
Montaña de los Riscos
Casas de las Montañas
Playa del Tambor
P. Eolico/Pol. Ind. Granadilla
Punta del Camello
Playa del Medio
Isidro/Granadilla
El Guirre
Punta del Tanque del Vidrio
Playa de la Rajita
Punta de la Pelada
Ensenada de la Pelada
Punta de los Mejillones
El Topo
El Médano
Punta del Médano
Playa del Médano
Punta del Bocinegro
Punta Roja

112

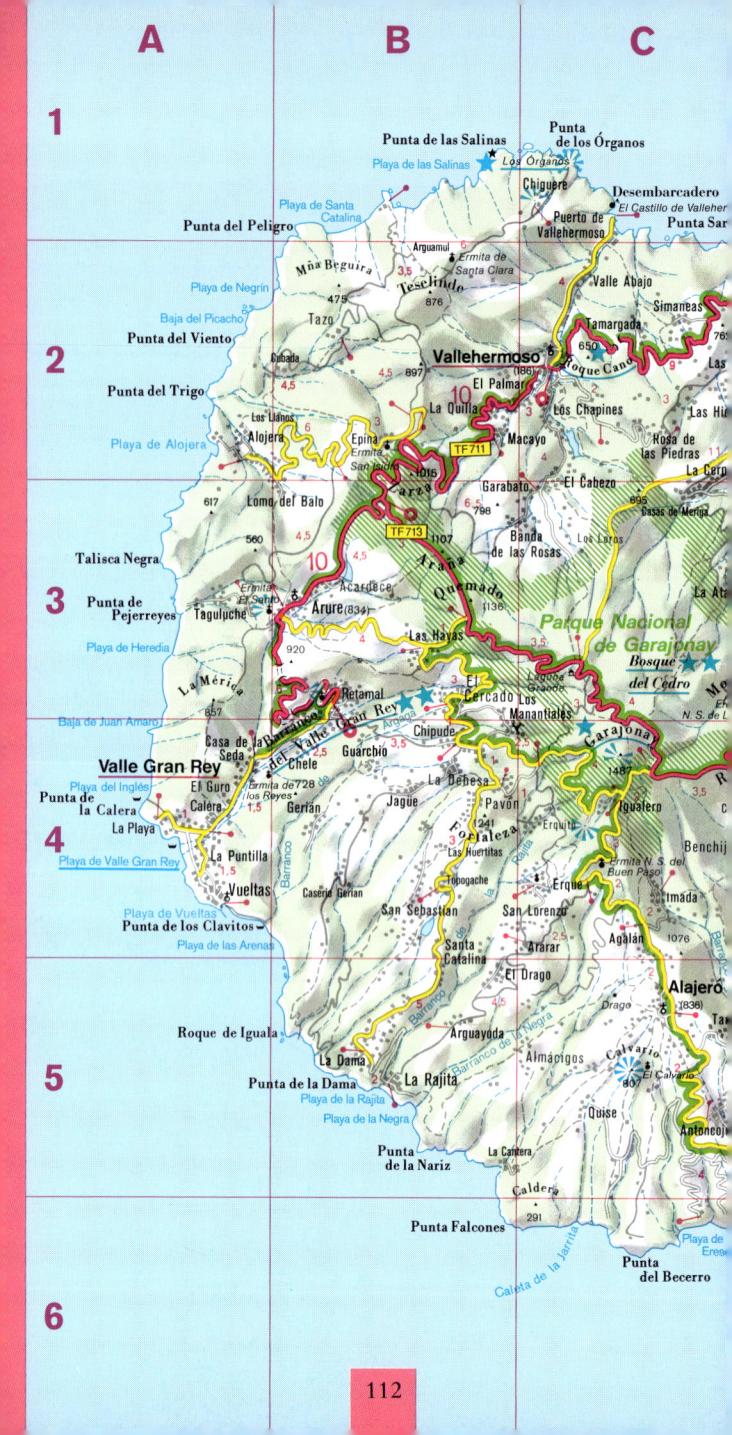

D
E
F
Gomera
1
2
3
4
5
6
Santa Cruz de la Palma 4 h
Punta del Jurado
Playa de San Marcos
Punta de Agulo
Las Casitas
Agulo
Playa de Agulo
Lepe
Playa de Sta. Catalina
Sta. Catalina
Punta Gabiña
El Tabaibal
Hermigua
San Juán
Playa de la Caleta
Altonazo
Punta San Lorenzo
Casas de la Caleta
Playa de los Incencios
Las Nuevitas
Casas del Palmar
Punta Palillos
Las Palmas
Casas del Álamo
Tagaluche
El Cabo
Barranco de Juel
Punta Majona
1065
Cueva Blancas
Punta Gaviota
Enchereda
620
Playa Zamora
El Rejo
634
48
Playa del Águila
956
Jaragán
Punta Llana
El Carmen
Ermita N. S. de Guadalupe
Ermita de Nuestra Señora de Guadalupe
Barranco
Jaragán
Playa del Cangrejo
Chejelipes
Lomito Fragoso y Honduras
642
1170
La Laja
Punta de Avalo
El Prado
TF711
El Molinito
Playa de Avalo
31
Matanza
Roca Bermeja
Punta de la Sabina
Tagamiche
Casas Blancas
San Antonio y Pilar
Parador Nacional
268
Vegaipala
692
Punta de San Cristóbal
979
Ayamosna
Iglesia de la Asunción
Jerduñe
TF713
(68)
La Costa
Torre del Conde
San Sebastián
1015
San Sebastián de la Gomera
864
430
Monum al Sagrado Corazón de Jesús
Playa de San Sebastian
Playa de Machal
Los Cristianos (Tenerife) 1¼ h
Seima
Pastrana
Tejiade
221
Playa de la Guancha
Cabezo
El Cabrito
Playa de El Cabrito
Contrera
Punta de El Cabrito
Barranco de Chinguarime
Playa de Oroja
Roque del Herrero
El Joradillo
Santiago
Playa de Suarez
Punta Gaviota
(109)
Santiago
Playa de Santiago
Punta Marichal
Playa de Santiago
Punta del Espino
Puerto de la Estaca (Hierro) 3 h

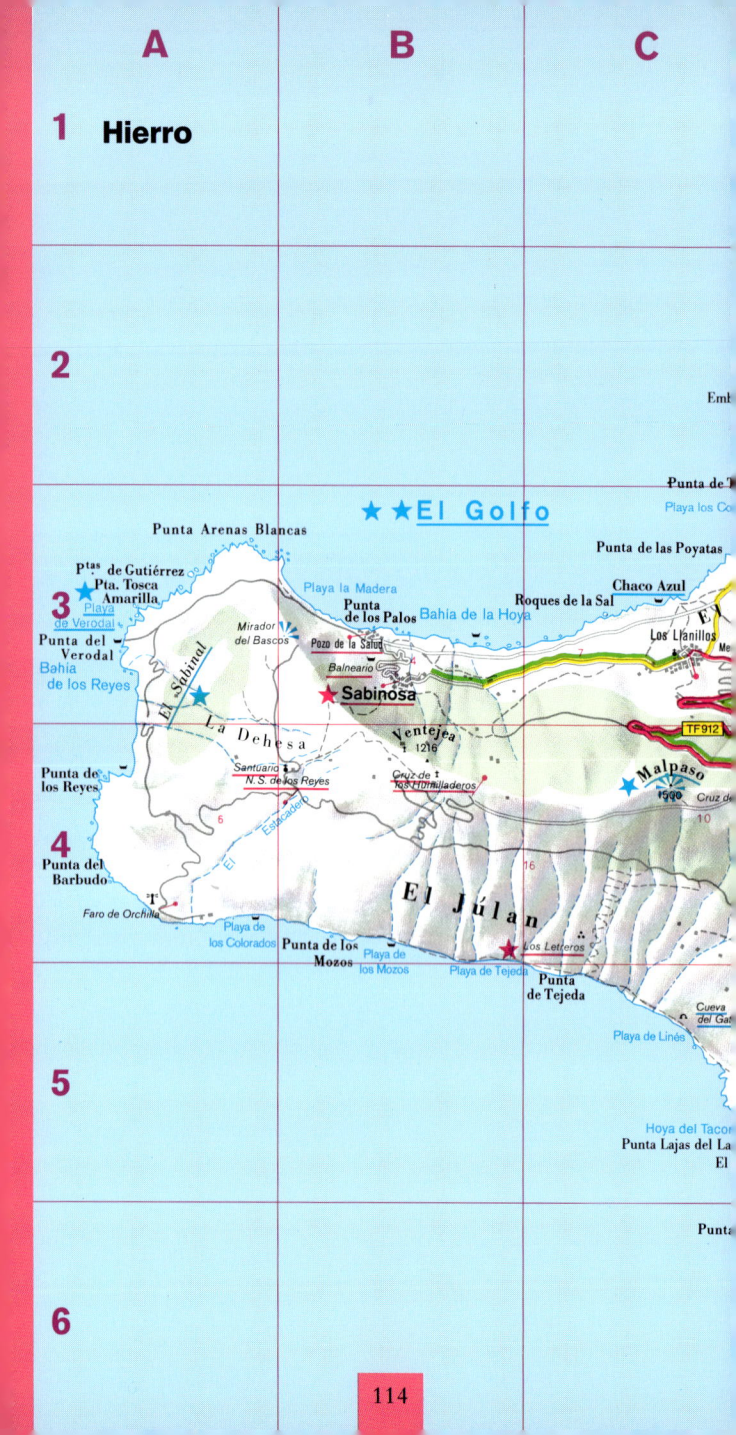

Hierro

★★ El Golfo

Punta Arenas Blancas
Punta de las Poyatas
Playa los Co...
Punta de T...

P^{tas} de Gutiérrez
Pta. Tosca Amarilla
Playa de Verodal
Punta del Verodal
Bahía de los Reyes
El Sabinal
Mirador del Bascos
Playa la Madera
Punta de los Palos
Bahía de la Hoya
Pozo de la Salud
Balneario
★ Sabinosa
Roques de la Sal
Chaco Azul
Los Llanillos
Me...

TF 912

La Dehesa
Santuario N.S. de los Reyes
Ventejea 1216
Cruz de los Humilladeros
Malpaso 1500
Cruz de

Punta de los Reyes
Estacabet...
El...
16
10

Punta del Barbudo

Faro de Orchila
Playa de los Colorados
Punta de los Mozos
Playa de los Mozos
Playa de Tejeda
Punta de Tejeda
Los Letteros
El Júlan
Cueva del Gat...
Playa de Linés

Hoya del Tacor...
Punta Lajas del La...
El

Punta

114

D
E
F
1
2
3
4
5
6
Punta del Guanche
Punta Norte
Bahía de las Calcosas
Las Salinas
Punta de Amacas
Pozo de las Calcosas
Echedo
Punta de Malpaís
Montaña Bermeja
345
Roque Salmor
Playa del Salto
Tamaduste
Ermita de San Pedro
Mocanal
Balneario
Ermita de San Lázaro
Aeropuerto de Hierro
Guarazoca
Betenama
Hoyo del Barrio
Alfoba
760
Playa del Cantadal
Erese
Valverde
(571)
Playas Largas
Mirador de la Peña
Jarales
Pedraje
La Caleta
Punta de la Caleta
Balneario
1023
Playa de la Caleta
Punta Grande
Las Montañetas
537
TF 911
1040
Barranco
Ribera
Santa Cruz de la Palma 4½ h
Las Casitas
Tiñor
Risco Tibataje
3,5
Chamuscada
Puerto de la Estaca
17
San Sebastián de la Gomera 3 h
Casas Gefnea
1232
1136
TF 912
Playa del Varadero
Izique
San Andrés
Playa de Tijeretas
Los Cristianos (Tenerife) 4½ h
Mocanes
Obelisca
San Telmo
Ermita de la Caridad
La Cuesta
Punta de Tijimiraque
Mirador de Jinama
Las Rosas
Las Lapas
(375)
Timbarombo
Frontera
1326
La Torre
Los Llanos
Belgara Alta
1371
Asomada
Tajace de Abajo
1118
Isora
Mirador de Bermeja
Punta de Ajones
Bermeja
Mirador de las Playas
25
Roques Bonanza
Punta de la Bonanza
Vivero Forestal
Las Playas
Hoya de Morcillo
Casa Forestal
Las Casas
Parador Nacional de El Hierro
1017
Mirador de Tanajara
Playa de los Cardones
Taibique
774
Punta de Miguel
Bahía de Miguel
Tembárgena
Playa Brava
Roques de los Joraditos
El Río
Gorona del Lajia
Playa de Manchas Blancas
El Lajial
Playa del Cantadal
Restinga
Punta del Miradero
197
La Restinga
Punta de la Restinga
Punta de los Saltos

Islas Canarias
(España)

A T L Á N T I C O

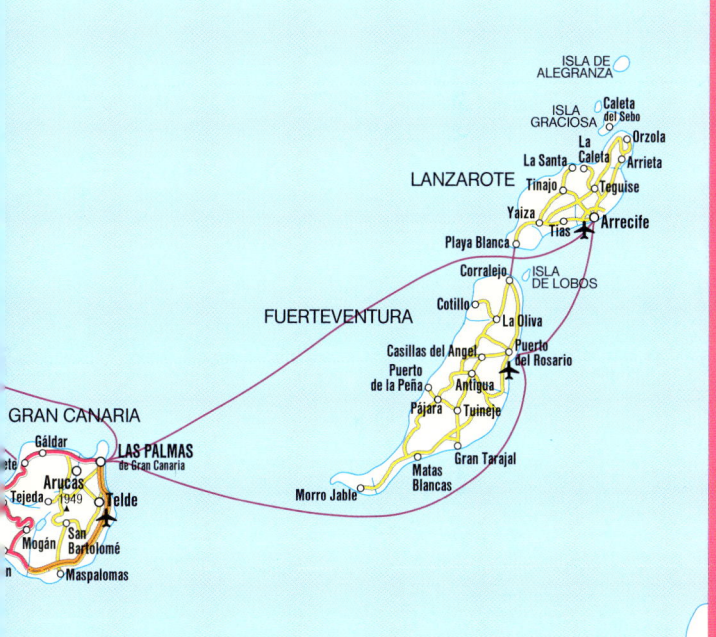

ISLA DE ALEGRANZA

ISLA GRACIOSA
Caleta del Sebo
Orzola
La Caleta
La Santa
Arrieta
Tinajo
Tequise
LANZAROTE
Yaiza
Tías
Arrecife
Playa Blanca
Corralejo
ISLA DE LOBOS
Cotillo
FUERTEVENTURA
La Oliva
Casillas del Angel
Puerto del Rosario
Puerto de la Peña
Antigua
Pájara
Tuineje
GRAN CANARIA
Gáldar
LAS PALMAS de Gran Canaria
Arucas
Tejeda 1949
Telde
Mogán
San Bartolomé
Gran Tarajal
Matas Blancas
Morro Jable
Maspalomas

Al-'Ayun (Lâayoune)
Lâayoune Plage

Sahara Occidental

Lemsid

ROAD ATLAS LEGEND

Autobahn mit Mautstelle und Anschlußstelle mit Nummer · Rasthaus mit Übernachtung · Raststätte · Erfrischungsstelle · Tankstelle · Parkplatz mit und ohne WC	Motorway with toll station and junction with number · Motel · Restaurant · Snackbar · Filling-station · Parking place with and without WC
Autobahn in Bau und geplant mit Datum der Verkehrsübergabe	Motorway under construction and projected with completion date
Zweibahnige Straße (4-spurig)	Dual carriageway (4 lanes)
Sonstige Kfz.-Straße	Road for motor vehicles only
Bundesstraße · Straßennummern	Federal road · Road numbers
Wichtige Hauptstraße	Important main road
Hauptstraße · Tunnel · Brücke	Main road · Tunnel · Bridge
Nebenstraßen	Minor roads
Fahrweg · Fußweg	Track · Footpath
Wanderweg (Auswahl)	Tourist footpath (selection)
Eisenbahn mit Fernverkehr	Main line railway
Zahnradbahn, Standseilbahn	Rack-railway, funicular
Kabinenschwebebahn · Sessellift	Aerial cableway · Chair-lift
Autofähre	Car ferry
Personenfähre	Passenger ferry
Schiffahrtslinie	Shipping route
Naturschutzgebiet · Sperrgebiet	Nature reserve · Prohibited area
Nationalpark, Naturpark · Wald	National park, natural park · Forest
Straße für Kfz gesperrt	Road closed to motor vehicles
Straße mit Gebühr	Toll road
Straße mit Wintersperre	Road closed in winter
Straße für Wohnanhänger gesperrt bzw. nicht empfehlenswert	Road closed or not recommended for caravans
Touristenstraße · Paß	Tourist route · Pass
Schöner Ausblick · Rundblick · Landschaftlich bes. schöne Strecke	Scenic view · Panoramic view · Route with beautiful scenery
Golfplatz · Schwimmbad	Golf-course · Swimming pool
Ferienzeltplatz · Zeltplatz	Holiday camp · Transit camp
Jugendherberge · Sprungschanze	Youth hostel · Ski jump
Kirche im Ort, freistehend · Kapelle	Churches · Chapel
Kloster · Klosterruine	Monastery · Monastery ruin
Schloß, Burg · Schloß-, Burgruine	Palace, castle · Ruin
Turm · Funk-, Fernsehturm	Tower · Radio-, TV-tower
Leuchtturm · Kraftwerk	Lighthouse · Power station
Wasserfall · Schleuse	Waterfall · Lock
Bauwerk · Marktplatz, Areal	Important building · Market place, area
Ausgrabungs- u. Ruinenstätte · Feldkreuz	Arch. excavation, ruins · Calvary
Dolmen · Menhir	Dolmen · Menhir
Hünen-, Hügelgrab · Soldatenfriedhof	Cairn · Military cemetary
Hotel, Gasthaus, Berghütte · Höhle	Hotel, inn, refuge · Cave

Kultur / **Culture**

German	Example	English
Malerisches Ortsbild · Ortshöhe	WIEN (171)	Picturesque town · Height of settlement
Eine Reise wert	★★ MILANO	Worth a journey
Lohnt einen Umweg	★ TEMPLIN	Worth a detour
Sehenswert	Andermatt	Worth seeing

Landschaft / **Landscape**

German	Example	English
Eine Reise wert	★★ Las Cañadas	Worth a journey
Lohnt einen Umweg	★ Texel	Worth a detour
Sehenswert	Dikti	Worth seeing

5 km
2,5 mi

INDEX

This index lists all the sites and places mentioned in this guide. Numbers in boldface refer to main entries, italics to photographs

Abama 73
Adeje 15, *27*, **81**
Aguamansa **45**, 63, 86, 95
Alcalá 73
Almáciga 58
Anaga massif 9, 15, 19, 51, 54, **58**, 95
Ángelestal (Valle de los Ángeles) 60
Arafo 67, **68**
Arenas Negras, Las **47**, 95
Arico **68**, 71
Aripe 83
Bajamar 33, **51**
Barranco del Infierno 82
Buenavista del Norte 21, 36, **45**, 48, 89
Cactus Park – Tenerife Zoo 74
Caleta, La 49, 73, **82**
Cañadas (del Teide), Las 19, 51, 59, **63**, 70, 86, 95, 96
Candelaria *16*, 31, 33, 55, **68**, 96
Cerrillar, Pico de 64
Chamorga 58, 95
Chayofita 74
Chinyero 15, 47
Chío 95
Chiqueros, Pico de 64
Chirche 83
Colmenas, Pico de 64
Cristianos, Los 7, 21, *28*, **73–76**, 77, 79, 84, 92, 96
Cruz Santa 95
Cueva del Hermano Pedro 78
Cueva del Viento 47
Cumbre Dorsal 8, 51, **58**, 67, 68, 87, 95
Cumbrilla, La 95
Esperanza, La 59, 88, 95
Fasnia 70
Galletas, Las **77**, 96
Garachico 31, 33, 35, 39, **45**, 48, 56, 89
Gigantes, Los **82**, *83*, 88, 96
Gomera (Island) 11, 74, 83, **84**, 88, 91, 96
Granadilla de Abona 21, **70**, 78
Guajara, Pico de 64
Guamasa 88
Guancha, La 21, 25, **46**
Guerra valley (Valle de Guerra) 51, **61**

Guía de Isora **83**, 92
Güímar 21, **67-68**, 70
Güímar valley (Valle de Güímar) **67**, 68
Hermanos, Dos (massif) 54
Hierro (Island) 11, 25, **85**
Icod el Alto 46
Icod de los Vinos *12*, 19, 21, 25, **47**, 48, *48*, 49, 89, 95
Isla Baja **36**, 45, 49
Laguna, La 6, 14, 17, 20, 21, 33, 51, **52**, 58, 59, 86, 95
Llanadas, Las 95
Lomo Bodegas 95
Masca 21, **48**, 88
Matanza de Acentejo, La 25, **53**, 60
Médano, El 71, **77**, 91
Mercedes, Las **58**, 95
Mirador de Don Martín 68
Mirador de Don Pompejo 45
Mirador de San Roque 71
Mirador Garachico 48
Mirador Humboldt 48
Montaña Blanca 65, 87
Montaña Grande 59
Montaña Roja 77
Montañeta, La **47**, 95
Naranjeros, Los 88
Orotava, La 14, 21, 31, 33, **36**, 39, 40, 48, 63, 86, 95
Orotava valley (Valle de la Orotava) 14, 15, 25, **35**, 36, 48, 67
Paisaje Lunar 70
Palo Blanco 95
Pico del Inglés 58
Playa de las Américas 7, *72*, 73, 74, **78–81**, 92, 94, 96
Playa de la Arena 83
Playa del Bobo 80
Playa Martiánez 39, **44**
Playa de San Juan 92
Playa de San Marcos 47, *48*, 89
Playa de Santiago 82, 88
Playa de las Teresitas 54, *55*
Playa de Troya 80
Poris de Abona 68, **71**, 96
Portillo, El 59, 63, 64, 65, 86, 87

Puertito de Sauzal 60
Puerto de la Cruz 10, 11, 14, 17, 23, 33, *34*, 35, **38–45**, 47, 63, 77, 86, 88, 91, 94, 95, 120
Puerto de Güímar **68**, 96
Puerto de Santiago 73, **83**, 88
Punta de Abona 68
Punta del Hidalgo 54
Punta de los Órganos 55
Punta de Teno 36, **48**, 89, 96
Radazul **59**, 96
Raíces, Las 88, 95
Rambleta, La 87
Realejos, Los 21, 25, 31, 46, **48**, 95
Reina Sofía (southern airport) 7, 38, **91**
Rodeos, Los (northern airport) 59, 85, 88, **91**
Roques, Los 95
San Andrés 21, **54**, 58, 95
San Juan 73, **83**
San Juan de la Rambla 21, 95
San Lorenzo valley (Valle de San Lorenzo) 78
San Miguel 78
Santa Cruz de Tenerife 6, 17, 31, 51, **55–58**, 59, 92, 94, 96, 97, 120
Santa Úrsula 25, 48, 51, **59**
Santiago del Teide 47, 48, **88**, 89
Sauzal, El 60
Silos, Los **49**, 89
Socorro, El 69
Tabaiba 59
Tabornó, Pico de 58
Tacoronte 25, 33, 51, **60**
Taganana 21, **58**, 95
Tanque, El 89
Teide, Pico del 6, 9, 15, 19, 35, 48, 58, *62*, **63**, 65, *67*, 84, 88, *90*
Tejina valley (Valle de Tejina) 51
Ten-Bel 76
Teno hills 9, 15, **36**, 45, 48, 82, 88
Topete 46
Valle de Guerra 51, **61**
Victoria de Acentejo, La 6, 25, **61**
Vilaflor 25, *66*, **71**, 95
Volcán de Fasnia 70

What do you get for your money?

Given the frequent fluctuations in exchange rates, it's impossible to say exactly what your money is worth in pesetas. You won't be far wrong in your estimates if you reckon on 237 ptas to the pound or 140 ptas to the dollar. If you take Eurocheques or Travellers' Cheques, then you tend to get a better exchange rate than for cash. A number of banks and exchange booths demand a high commission, so it's a good idea to shop around for the best rate. The Spanish currency is the peseta. There are coins in denominations of 1 pta, 5 ptas, 25 ptas, 50 ptas, 100 ptas, 200 ptas and 500 ptas, and notes of 1,000 ptas, 2,000 ptas, 5,000 ptas and 10,000 ptas. Prices vary greatly between the tourist regions and the rural villages. Here are a few examples: a coffee *(café con leche)* in Playa de las Américas will cost between 125 and 200 ptas, while in the interior it won't cost much more than 100 ptas; a bottle of beer in a simple bar might set you back 125-150 ptas, in a restaurant it will be 300 ptas; a bus trip from Puerto de la Cruz to Santa Cruz de Tenerife costs 750 ptas. Museum admissions cost up to 500 ptas, but many are free. Simple set meals range from 900-1,200 ptas, while a paella for two costs between 1,600 and 2,000 ptas. The chart below will help you to make quick conversions, but for more exact and up-to-date rates you should check in the paper or bank before cashing.

US$	Spanish pesetas (pts)	£	Spanish pesetas (pts)	Can$	Spanish pesetas (pts)
1	139	1	237	1	90
2	279	2	474	2	181
3	418	3	711	3	271
4	557	4	948	4	361
5	696	5	1,185	5	451
10	1,393	10	2,370	10	903
15	2,089	15	3,600	15	1,354
20	2,786	20	4,740	20	1,805
25	3,482	25	5,925	25	2,257
30	4,178	30	7,110	30	2,708
40	5,571	40	9,480	40	3,611
50	6,964	50	11,850	50	4,514
60	8,357	60	14,219	60	5,416
70	9,750	70	16,589	70	6,319
80	11,142	80	18,959	80	7,222
90	12,535	90	21,329	90	8,124
100	13,928	100	23,699	100	9,027
200	27,856	200	47,398	200	18,054
300	41,784	300	71,097	300	27,081
400	55,712	400	94,796	400	36,108
500	69,640	500	118,495	500	45,135
750	104,460	750	177,743	750	67,703
1000	139,280	1000	336,990	1000	90,270